Twayne's United States Authors Series

Sylvia E. Bowman, *Editor*

INDIANA UNIVERSITY

Cornelius Mathews

Cornelius Mathews

By ALLEN F. STEIN

North Carolina State University

Twayne Publishers, Inc.   ::   New York

ISBN 0-8057-0478-7

MANUFACTURED IN THE UNITED STATES OF AMERICA

For
Gale, Philip, and Wendy

Preface

Although today Cornelius Mathews is little more than a name encountered in footnotes or in specialized studies like Perry Miller's *The Raven and the Whale* (1956) and John Paul Pritchard's *Literary Wise Men of Gotham* (1963), he was in his own day a well-known and controversial author and critic whose single-minded advocacy of the cause of American literary nationalism won him some support and many enemies. Essentially, his campaign for a distinctly American literature was a twofold effort in that he was both a propagandist, delivering speeches and writing essays calling for American literary independence and for the international copyright law that he believed would hasten its coming, and a creative writer who attempted in his own work to show what a native literature ought to be.

My purpose is to deal specifically with Mathews' writings, particularly those of his major period of creativity, 1835–56, and to examine the manner in which he used the native materials he claimed could be the basis for a vital national literature. Such a close study of Mathews' work has not heretofore been attempted; as a result, those of us who know of Mathews at all are probably more acquainted with his personality, as Miller depicts it, than with his books and the valuable commentary they make on the American scene. For the most part, I shall leave discussion of the literary background of the era, with its numerous feuds, cliques, and rival theories, to Miller and Pritchard, and to two other helpful works, John Stafford's *The Literary Criticism of Young America* (1952) and Sidney Moss's *Poe's Literary Battles* (1963), in order that my study of Mathews' writings will not be obscured by the morass of personal animosities permeating New York literary life one hundred and twenty-five years ago.

A national literature, as Mathews envisioned it, would serve as a continuing source of inspiration for the American people, while articulating their ideals and traditions. In "The Poet" he describes, in terms much like Ralph Waldo Emerson's, the role the

American writer must assume:

> Gather all kindreds of this boundless realm
>   To speak a common tongue in thee! be thou—
> Heart, pulse and voice, whether pent hate o'erwhelm
>   The stormy speech or young love whisper low.
> Cheer them, immitigable battle-drum!
>   Forth, truth-mailed, to the old unconquered field—
> And lure them gently to a laurelled home,
>   In notes softer than lutes or viols yield.
> Fill all the stops of life with tuneful breath,
> Closing their lids, bestow a dirge-like death![1]

In endeavoring to carry out this role, Mathews depicted events of American history as if they were part of a vast national epic and described typical local scenes in an effort to show his countrymen how grand, exciting, and colorful American life and a literary treatment of it could be. Also, he served as a critic of American failures and shortcomings, describing and attacking political corruption, social injustice, and other departures from our democratic traditions and values.

Each major segment of Mathews' work as it relates to literary nationalism or to his observations of the American scene will be studied in a separate chapter. This plan will, of course, entail some overlapping, with some works appearing in several chapters and being studied from different angles; but it will, hopefully, enable me to avoid undue repetition, while, at the same time, allowing me to provide an overall picture of Mathews' depiction and criticism of American life.

ALLEN F. STEIN

North Carolina State University

Acknowledgments

Because all of Mathews' work is long out of print, and few of his books are extant, it was necessary to acquire microfilms of the Mathews holdings in the New York Public Library. I am grateful to the Duke University Library for making these acquisitions and for enabling me to obtain additional Mathews works through its interlibrary loan service. I am also indebted to the New York Public Library and to the Houghton Library of Harvard University for granting me access to letters and manuscripts of Cornelius Mathews.

I also wish to express my appreciation to Professors Arlin Turner, Bernard Duffey, and Victor Strandberg of Duke University, who read and provided helpful criticism of my doctoral dissertation on Cornelius Mathews, upon which much of this book is based. Finally, my greatest debt is to my wife Gale, who was a constant aid in the preparation of this study.

Contents

Chronology

CHAPTER 1

Mathews and His Era

I *"A Small Man in Glasses"*

CORNELIUS Mathews was born October 28, 1817, at his grandfather's estate in Port Jefferson, a small town near Lake Rye
in Westchester County, not far from New York, the city to which
he moved as a boy and which he grew to love. He was the second
son of Abijah Mathews, "a prominent New Yorker of the best
type,"[1] and Catherine Van Cott, who belonged to one of the oldest
Knickerbocker families of New York. On the paternal side, his
ancestry was Welsh and in this country went back to Ananias
Mathews, one of the earlier settlers of Long Island. Although
Cornelius rarely left New York City, except for short outings, he
evidently always remembered with pleasure the countryside at his
grandfather's home, as is frequently noted in the idyllic descriptions
of rural scenes that occur in his writing.

Mathews attended Columbia University in 1830 and 1831, trans-
ferring in 1832 to New York University, of which his relative,
Daniel Mathews, was the first president. Mathews entered in the
second class of the new school and graduated in July, 1834, in the
university's first commencement exercise. At that ceremony
Mathews delivered an address entitled "Females of the American
Revolution," which revealed an interest in American history which
stayed with him throughout his life. Later, he became the first
president of the Alumni Association of the university. In 1837
Mathews, satisfying his father's wishes, became a lawyer, but it
is apparent that he looked on his new career with apprehension.
In a letter to his friend George Duyckinck he wrote sardonically
of the law: "Goddess of Justice: thou Wooden Equity that sur-
mounted the dome, who with thy timber cerebellum presidest
over the forensic orgies and revels that go on beneath; I station
myself before your Carpenter-Created majesty and bow, with pro-
foundest awe and misgivings and doubts."[2] Mathews' fears seem
to have been realized, for he wrote George Duyckinck two years

later, describing himself as a "plodding lawyer" working on petty cases as a minor member of a large firm.[3] Indeed, Mathews seems never to have reconciled himself fully to his law career and finally gave it up altogether in the late 1840's.

In the late 1830's and early 1840's Mathews increasingly devoted himself to literature rather than to law; and he published numerous works, including, among others, *Our Forefathers, Behemoth,* "The True Aims of Life," and *The Career of Puffer Hopkins.* These works manifest his concern with literary nationalism and with the American scene in general—topics which interested him greatly throughout his life. By the conclusion of his career, Mathews had devoted himself to the treatment of these topics in diverse literary endeavors, which included the writing of poetry, plays, tales, sketches, novels, and essays, as well as in addresses, lectures, and sermons. He was also the first American editor of the works of Elizabeth Barrett Browning. In addition to his literary work, Mathews led an active civic life; he was nominated to the New York State legislature at the age of twenty; and he served as a church trustee and as a member of the board of directors of a museum.[4]

His period of greatest literary creativity was between 1835 and 1856, when all of his important work was produced. In these years Mathews devoted himself most energetically to the cause of American literary nationalism, originating the "Young America" party and founding the American Copyright Club.[5] In his efforts on behalf of a national literature he was closely associated with Evert and George Duyckinck, editors of several New York literary journals and compilers of the *Cyclopaedia of American Literature;* William Cullen Bryant; Francis Hawks, a New York man of letters; John L. O'Sullivan, fiery editor of the *United States Magazine and Democratic Review;* William Arthur Jones, the critic; Herman Melville; William Gilmore Simms; and others. Also during these years the vehemency of Mathews' propagandizing on behalf of the liberal cause of literary nationalism led him to incur the enmity of the powerful Lewis Gaylord Clark, editor of the influential *Knickerbocker* magazine, a literary journal of generally conservative, Whiggish sympathies. For more than a decade, Cornelius Mathews was a familiar character in the pages of the *Knickerbocker* and like-minded periodicals, for he became a convenient butt for the humor and scorn of Clark and his wide circle of literary friends.

However unpalatable Mathews' ideas of literary nationalism may have been to many of his contemporaries, his frequently abrasive personality was even more instrumental in establishing him as the target for the many severe attacks he endured. A pompous and vain man, Mathews is remembered today only "as [one] who excited among his contemporaries a frenzy of loathing beyond the limits of rationality." He was short and heavy-set, "wore small steel-rimmed spectacles, bounced when he talked, walked the streets of New York with a strut that nothing could dismay, and delivered himself in an oracular jargon designed to drive all good fellows either to drink or profanity."[6]

Inspired by his consummate self-assurance, Mathews devoted himself to the campaign for literary nationalism, of which he considered himself chief spokesman. Too often, however, in this role he blundered into situations in which his habitual tactlessness and conceit led him to damage inadvertently the cause for which he worked. As we shall see in Chapter 2, Mathews seized the occasion, in 1842, of the dinner in New York City for Charles Dickens, to launch into a long tirade advocating the passage of an international copyright law, which, its proponents believed, would greatly aid in the development of a native American literature. While such a law would have benefited Dickens himself, whose works were frequently at the mercy of piratical American publishers, it seems that he and everybody else at the dinner, lulled into mellow spirits by good food and drink, and by short, pleasant speeches lionizing the British visitor, had little patience for Mathews' long harangue. In fact, Mathews is described by Perry Miller as "speaking against the din." Furthermore, if his words had been heard, they would have done little but unsettle the digestive processes of the listeners; for Mathews had no compunction about declaring at this dinner that copyright would "awe into everlasting silence the brood of maggot-pies, and buzzards, and carrion vultures that now obstruct the light, and spreading their obscene chittering wings before the eyes of the people, shut the clear heaven from the view."[7] The timing of this speech and similarly mishandled efforts made Mathews seem to many an annoying and ludicrous figure; and, unfortunately, he tended to make the cause he represented seem ludicrous as well.

James Russell Lowell, hitting at Mathews' conceit and at his increasing tendency to see all criticism leveled at him and his work as a veiled attack on the cause he represented, created a characterization of him in *A Fable for Critics* which Clark and other New York observers believed to be an extremely accurate one. Lowell presented Mathews as a suspicious, envious, and vindictive little man:

> a small man in glasses
> Went dodging about, muttering, "Murderers! asses!"
> From out of his pocket a paper he'd take,
> With the proud look of martyrdom tied to its stake,
> And, reading a squib at himself, he'd say, "Here I see
> 'Gainst American letters a bloody conspiracy,
> They are all by my personal enemies written;
> I must post an anonymous letter to Britain,
> And show that this gall is the merest suggestion
> Of spite at my zeal on the Copyright question,
> For, on this side the water, 'tis prudent to pull
> O'er the eyes of the public their national wool,
> By accusing of slavish respect to John Bull
> All American authors who have more or less
> Of that anti-American humbug—success. . . ."[8]

Indeed, Mathews seemed, ultimately, to have even had a falling-out with his long-time friends and protectors, the Duyckincks. In 1852, in a letter to Evert, Mathews claimed that the brothers had treated him shabbily by not allowing him the opportunity to make the first offer for the *Literary World,* the weekly review and critical journal which they were in the process of selling. It was, Mathews asserted, largely on the strength of discussions with the Duyckincks several years before, regarding the possibility of running a literary journal with them, that he was led "to abandon the Law which [he] was practising successfully." Mathews' subsequent exclusion from any interest in the *Literary World,* which "without any action on [his] part was substituted" for the proposed journal, entitled him, he believed, to special consideration now that the Duyckincks were disposing of their periodical.[9] It is difficult, however, to credit Mathews' sense of grievance. First, his implication that the Duyckincks virtually beguiled him into leaving a thriving law practice belies the facts, for Mathews was clearly unhappy in this profession and was not temperamentally suited to make a success of it. Further, it is doubtful that Mathews could have come up with the funds to buy the *Literary World*. Indeed, as recently as 1849 and 1850 he had written several letters to Evert in which he urgently asked to borrow small sums of money and begged for work on the *Literary World* for which he might get some return, however small. Obviously not the betrayer Mathews' letter implies him to be, Duyckinck always complied with these requests. Finally, Mathews' failures in the late 1840's in several ventures on his own as magazine editor would have made it extremely difficult for him to find the financial backing which his own shortage of funds would have made necessary. The intemperate letter to the Duyckincks, therefore, serves merely to show that the unflattering picture one receives of Mathews may often have been a well-earned one.

By the middle 1850's few took Mathews seriously even as a nuisance, and whatever influence he may have had on the literary thinking of his era was gone. He wrote little of consequence and drifted into relative obscurity, after the 1850's, writing, as a rule anonymously, for second-rate journals.[10] His last position, which he held from 1882 until his death in 1889, was contributing editor of the *New York Dramatic Mirror,* a nondescript journal of theater news. During his last years, he lived in semiretirement, making weekly visits to the *Mirror*'s offices to catch up on the news, saying, as he sat surrounded by piles of newspapers at his desk, that he was "in his observatory, surveying mankind."[11] Scanning the national scene was his practice throughout his long life; and it is as a record of salient observations on mid-nineteenth-century America that his work has its significance.

II *An American Literature*

Mathews' effort to create a body of writing relevant to the American scene was based on the belief, which he held in common with many of his contemporaries, that for America to thrive spiritu-ally and intellectually it must have a literature that would not merely imitate English authors and look to English critics for approval but would deal with American themes and the American landscape; and if, perchance, it treated a foreign subject, would look at it from the fresh vantage point of the New World. Although such writers as James Kirke Paulding, William Ellery Channing, John Neal, William Cullen Bryant, and James Fenimore Cooper were instrumental during the late 1810's and the 1820's in establishing for the first time in America a genuine awareness of the need for a literature reflective of American ideals, it was not until the twenty-five years immediately preceding the Civil War that the call for literary nationalism reached its peak. Clearly, Emerson's declaration in 1837 in "The American Scholar" that "we have listened too long to the courtly muses of Europe," represented the beliefs of a greater number of people than would have been true ten years earlier.

Probably contributing in large part to the increased popularity of literary nationalism in the 1830's were the aggressively democratic tendencies and occasional jingoism engendered by the age of Jackson, factors which would add sanction to any effort to provide a "Home-Literature," such as Mathews demanded. Certainly, O'Sullivan's *United States Magazine and Democratic Review,* with which Mathews, Evert Duyckinck, William Arthur Jones, and Walt Whitman were all associated, was from 1837 until the middle 1840's a fervent spokesman for "Americanism." Similarly, "Young America" was a visionary political movement as well as a literary one. Whatever their political ties, however, most American writers from the middle 1830's until the Civil War felt the need to deal with American materials and to encourage their compatriot writers to do the same.

Thus, such "Young Americans" as Mathews, Duyckinck, Jones, and others, felt that they were responding to a national demand when they advocated the establishment of a literature that would both articulate the needs and ideals of the American people and provide them with inspiration. In this vein, Duyckinck described what an American literature ought to entail: "First and foremost, nationality involves the idea of home writers. Secondly, the choice of a due proportion of home themes, affording opportunity for descriptions of our scenery, for the illustration of passing events, and the preservation of what tradition has rescued from the past, and for the exhibition of the manners of the people, and the circumstances which give form and pressure to the time and the spirit of the country; and all of these penetrated and vivified by an intense and enlightened patriotism."[12]

William Arthur Jones, in a series of articles entitled "Democracy and Literature" for the *Democratic Review* in 1842, spoke of "Poetry for the People"; and his remarks reveal much of what the Young Americans believed should be the function of a nation's writing with regard to its people. Showing his awareness of the spirit of the times, Jones claimed that the "predominant fact" in the history of the nineteenth century was the rise of the people. In order to respond to the new situation and to keep their work from becoming dessicated, American poets, he stated, must write for the people and teach them the lessons of relevance to the world in which they live. Consequently, Jones urged the American poet to write of "the necessity and dignity of labor," the "native nobility of an honest and brave heart," the uselessness of "conventional distinctions of rank and wealth," the necessity of maintaining an "honorable poverty and a contented spirit," and finally "the brotherhood and equality of man." Jones concluded by looking forward to the day when America would have its "Homer of the Mass."[13]

If a writer aimed at speaking to the people, most of the Young Americans believed, the world he showed them would have to be depicted in a realistic manner. Genius, declared Duyckinck, in *Arcturus,* the literary journal which he co-edited with Mathews, finds in common things more than common men find; and anyone clearsighted enough to give a true picture of actual life must produce a great book. True imagination is manifested by conveying the full consciousness of reality and in doing simple justice to the characters and events of actual life, which means, in large part, having a sympathy with the actors and placing oneself in their situation. As Pritchard points out, Duyckinck shows here the obvious influence of Wordsworth, and he "furnishes a bridge from Wordsworth to Whitman of which the latter took full advantage."[14]

With a new realism in depicting the national life would assuredly come, the literary nationalists thought, an American humor that might capture the spirit of the American people and be commensurate with their imagination, color, and vitality. Duyckinck called upon American humorists to "separate the true qualities of a man from the common-places that surround him, and illustrate life by the contrast between a soul such as nature made it, and society in its thousand abuses reflects it." He believed that they should satirize man for his foibles and errors, but look at him with compassion also, for there are "traits of divinity even in the infirmities of our nature." He saw the ultimate goal of comedy as not merely to make us laugh but to give us hope and encouragement as well. Furthermore, like poetry, humor is an attempt "to accommodate the shows of the world to the desires of the mind."[15] These were views in which Mathews strongly concurred and which he tried to put into practice in his writing.

Others who were neither Young Americans nor enthusiastic literary nationalists, believed that a democratic literature "for the people" was either dangerous or impossible. Longfellow, in *Kavanaugh,* humorously caricatured a literary nationalist, making him seem an opportunistic semibarbarian who had little understanding of what great literature entails. Longfellow, as Lowell was to do later, advocated the establishment of a natural rather than national literature. Similarly, Holmes, in his "Astraea: The Balance of Illusions," presents a vociferous Manhattan literary nationalist whose chauvinistic bombast only reveals his pathetic provincialism.

More vitriolic, however, in their attacks on the literary nationalists and their program were such New Yorkers as Clark and others who wrote for Clark's *Knickerbocker* or for the *Whig Review.* The animus of Clark and his circle toward the Young Americans was both literary and political. First of all, the nationalists objected to the kind of imitative literature that Clark's friends wrote; second, they objected, with Poe, to Clark's practice of "puffing," or lavishing indiscriminate praise on a friend or a contributor to his magazine. (Ostensibly in retaliation, though, E. A. Duyckinck, Mathews, Simms, and their associates frequently indulged in "puffing.") Moreover, it seems that the Clark group, while nominally in favor of a native literature, in practice usually praised books imitative of English authors and frowned on anything akin to the rough, shaggy literature desired by the nationalists. They were opposed to this kind of writing because, essentially, they were conservatives who could not tolerate anything approaching a barbaric yawp, whether esthetic, intellectual, or political. If literary barriers were torn down, they thought, social barriers would fall next. Because of this disapproval, Mathews' self-assured, vociferous calls for Young Americanism aroused their ire and led to the attacks which made Mathews a controversial figure.

III *Teaching by Example*

Mathews' work on behalf of the aims of the literary nationalists falls into two major parts: his explicit propaganda calling for a home literature, and his effort to show in his own creative writing the role an American writer should play as a spokesman for his compatriots. In his novels, plays, sketches, tales, and poems he provided pictures of American life to convey to his readers a sense of the qualities which make their life peculiarly an American one. He attempted to show them that their nation was one of which they could be proud and that the principles which gave it being were still worthy of admiration and emulation. To this end, he endeavored to remind his countrymen of their nation's heroic past and of the vitality, spirit, and humor which still permeated the national scene. However, he did not neglect some of the more unpleasant aspects of the American experience; in great part, his works are a commentary on the failures and shortcomings which often belie our traditions and principles.

Mathews' earliest significant works, the tales and sketches collected in *The Motley Book* (1838), are colorful vignettes of New York, calculated to provide a picture of life in the city and its environs, which Mathews believed to be representative of the nation at large. Often satirical, these scenes are early examples of the more far-reaching social commentary that Mathews was to make later. The picture of New York City life was expanded in 1850 in *The Prompter*, Mathews' magazine of theater news, and in *A Pen-and-Ink Panorama of New York City*, in which Mathews, serving as tour guide, takes his readers around the city, showing its colorful sights.

Behemoth: A Legend of the Mound-builders (1839) and *Wakondah* (1841), dealing with the prehistoric Indians who inhabited the American continent, are attempts to create an epic showing the heroism which even ages ago made America a land marked for greatness. Also dealing with the heroic American past are: *Witchcraft* (1846), a poetic drama of the Salem witch trials, portraying the courage of a mother and son who resisted the hysteria; *Big Abel and the Little Manhattan* (1845), an epic presentation of contemporary New York City and its earlier courageous inhabitants, the Indians and the Dutch; and *Chanticleer* (1850), a tale of a representative American family's Thanksgiving holiday, in which the main character, the patriarch of the family, is an aged Revolutionary War veteran, who serves as a visible reminder of the nation's heroic past. (A tragic drama, *Jacob Leisler, The Patriot Hero, or, New York in 1690,* dealing with a colonial rebellion, was produced in 1848, but no copy is extant.) In later years Mathews returned to the American past in *The Indian Fairy Book* (1856), reissued in 1869 as *The Enchanted Moccasins.* This work is a retelling, with only the slightest changes in wording, of Indian legends collected by Henry Schoolcraft.

Describing the American follies and evils which betray her heroic past are Mathews' novel of city life, *The Career of Puffer Hopkins* (1842); his satiric drama, *The Politicians* (1840); and many of the topical sketches in Mathews' humor magazines, *Yankee Doodle* (1846–47), and its sequel, *The Elephant* (1848). All of these make satirical attacks on the corruption and demagoguery which impede the orderly processes of the American political system. Also, *Puffer Hopkins, Big Abel and the Little Manhattan,* and *Yankee Doodle* portray something of the unpleasantness of life in the lower depths of New York society. Similarly, *Moneypenny, or, The Heart of the World* (1849), a satirical mystery novel; *False Pretences* (1856), a comic play; and *Chanticleer* all portray a crisis in American values and manners. In *Calmstorm, The Reformer* (1853), a poetic drama; *Puffer Hopkins; Poems on Man* (1845); and several articles in *Arcturus* (the critical journal which Mathews edited with E. A. Duyckinck in 1841 and 1842); and in *Yankee Doodle,* Mathews describes the problem of social injustice in American life and evolves a social philosophy to deal with it— one that emphasizes the virtues of the American past which he loved since he advocates a return to the principles of honesty and individualism to which the founders of the nation had adhered.

We see, then, that Mathews attempted to serve as a mediator who might revivify an often decadent present by transmitting to it a sense of the past. Therefore, he had to make his countrymen aware of the contemporary situation and, at the same time, to juxtapose it to a more heroic and noble past in order that a renewed present might evolve into a glorious future. He put his faith in a national literature as a means of insuring this brighter future, and he dedicated his life to the cause of its development.

CHAPTER 2

Mathews' Support of Literary Nationalism

I *True Aims of an American Author*

I N the late 1830's and through the 1840's, particularly in New York City, the call for a distinctly American literature and for an international copyright law that its proponents believed would aid immeasurably in the development of such a literature was at its loudest and most controversial. J. L. O'Sullivan's jingoistic *Democratic Review,* in which the phrase "Manifest Destiny" first appeared, was a leading force for literary nationalism, as were the *American Monthly Magazine* from 1835 to 1837 under Charles Fenno Hoffman, the *Arcturus* of Mathews and Evert Duyckinck, and the *Literary World* under the Duyckinck brothers. Among the New York writers at the time who frequently called for a "home" literature were Evert Duyckinck, William A. Jones, Herman Melville, and, perhaps most vociferously of all, Cornelius Mathews.

In 1839, in an address "The True Aims of Life," delivered before the alumni of New York University, Mathews provides a general statement of his ideals and reveals some of the reasons for his desire for a national literature. He declares that "to accomplish the true aims of life we must first know what our nature is and what it requires."[1] The high function of literature is to teach us to transform our human nature from "a rude, misshapen, unformed chaos of moral, intellectual, and physical ingredients into a work of symmetry and beauty" (9). Furthermore, "the vast reach, the towering strength and altitude of our nature and its capacity of extension, we know . . . has been the laborious duty of a long life in some men" (10). Not the least important of such men are the writers, for it is through them that "we can grasp the remote, the future, the past—that is above and beneath us and far off beyond the range of sense" (13). Mathews then speaks at length of the role that literature plays as an educative and moral force, claiming that "It is by literature that we . . . enlarge and elevate our vision" and "learn what human nature has been, what it is, and what it should be" (13).

Moreover, literature teaches us to regard every object with interest and "to feel that nothing about us is beneath our attention and cannot contribute to rational enjoyment" (15). Thus, we can learn from, and be inspired by, common, everyday objects as well as by those that are unusual. As Mathews was to declare in other works, very often the familiar objects, close at hand, have more to tell us than those remote ones which, because of the body of tradition behind them and their inherent snob appeal, seem to be invested with an aura of significance.

Mathews sounds a note of nationalism in this address, which, although used generally here, would be more closely applied to literature in later works. He states, "a sincere and earnest attachment to the land of our birth is calculated to awaken the whole soul into healthy action . . . and by casting a charm around the scene in which we dwell, impart to our nature a genial excitement under which its best powers are exerted" (26). In later speeches and essays Mathews claimed that a purely American literature would be the best means possible of fostering this salubrious communal feeling.

Mathews tells his audience that he sees in America's midst "a few chosen spirits" to whom has fallen "the custody of principles vital to the best interests of mankind. Scorned, slandered, ridiculed, it is their generous labor to hold up the banner of some outcast truth, and carry it forward amidst the clamors of an ignorant and passionate multitude" (33). Too often, though, as Mathews stated throughout the 1840's, such upholders of an outcast truth are not even heard because of the flood of foreign works into this country, which keeps many American works, except for potboilers, from being published.

For an American work to find a publisher and to attain even a modest financial success it must, according to Mathews, be one which is crassly imitative of English models. He attacks the situation in the preface to his satirical play, *The Politicians* (1840), in which he calls it "impertinent" to produce at American theaters "a constant succession of farces with Sir Harry Humdrum, my Lord Noddy, and my Lady Highdiddlediddle, attended by flying squads of waiters in livery and coachmen in topboots—to the entire exclusion of a single scene or personage that has the recommendation of fitness, either in respect to time, place, or audience."[2] The only Americans seen on an American stage are those whose characters are drawn by English playwrights. Mathews believes that any manager looks upon a manuscript of an American play with "about the same favor as he would peruse the washbook of one of his supernumeraries." Such treatment often leads native writers away from American subjects and the American landscape; therefore, the "rolling rivers, green dark woods, boundless meadows and majestic peaks" go unsung, and American ideals are unarticulated. Similarly, in his article "What Has Mr. Edwin Forrest Done For The American Drama?," Mathews derides the great actor for never having worked to encourage the growth of a genuinely national drama; instead, Forrest became a success by popularizing foreign plays and imitative American ones. Forrest contributed, as a result, to the establishment of conditions in which American tastes are so unformed or insecure that an actress of the caliber of Charlotte Cushman had to attain success in England before she could find acceptance in her own country, which previously ignored her.[3]

II *An Unpaid Literature*

Mathews believed that copyright agreement between the United States and England would significantly reduce the number of English books imported into this nation and thereby assure American writers a better chance to find a publisher and an audience among their own countrymen. As early as 1838, therefore, Mathews campaigned for the passage of such an agreement, having his supposititious author of *The Motley Book,* "the late Ben Smith," declare on his deathbed, "don't for heaven's sake risk it [his book] against the rabble of foreign publications, till that riot act is read in the presence of the mob."[4] Mathews' first major examination of the problems engendered by the lack of international copyright occurred, however, at the testimonial dinner for Charles Dickens on February 19, 1842, in his "A Speech on International Copyright," in which he describes the pernicious effects of the lack of a copyright agreement on American letters.

American writers, forced to compete with the unpaid foreign literature flooding their country, do not have a chance, says Mathews, of achieving the economic well-being which might spur them on to greater efforts: "Instead of being fostered and promoted, as it should be, our domestic literature is borne down by an un-

methodical and unrestrained republication of every foreign work
that will bear the charges of the composition and paper-maker."[5]

Mathews laments a condition in which a worthy English book
which merits American publication and a good sale is grabbed by a
score of piratically inclined publishers who produce different editions
and leave numerous American books unpublished. Even worse is
the situation which occurs when the English book is worthless but
is published and assured a good sale merely because it is English.
This piracy, certainly unfair to British authors, is more unfair to
American writers because the Englishman at least has a large following in his own nation, while the American can at best find only a
small one in the United States. Thus, a Charles Dickens is honored
and feted by Americans, while their native writers can usually be
found in "cramped and narrow" rooms, "poor, neglected, borne
down by the heavy hand of their country, laid like an oppressor's
hand upon them" (9). Mathews compares the American writer's
situation with that of his farmer compatriots, and he visualizes each
as coming down the Hudson River to New York City with his
produce. While the farmer gets a fair return for his crop and can
be found celebrating in a comfortable restaurant, the writer must
frantically run about the city from publishing house to publishing
house with his product and face repeated rejection because the
publishers are so busy pirating foreign works that leave no time
for consideration of his book (11).

Just as miserable as the plight of the author in a nation with no
international copyright agreement is that of the American public
at large, for the public taste is so deeply affected by the commercially
inspired laudations of inferior authors by publishers that the value
of literary reputation, as well as literary property, is greatly im-
paired. No distinction is made between good writers and bad because of the publishers' practice of "puffing," or writing unreservedly
laudatory reviews; and "the judgement of the general reader is so
perplexed that he cannot choose between Mr. Dickens and Mr.
Harrison Ainsworth—between the classical drama of Talfourd and
the vapid farce of Boucicault" (12). Not only is the American reading public flooded with bad books which are foisted upon it under
the guise of masterpieces, but it cannot even be sure that the
books it gets are those that the authors actually wrote because the
piratical publishers operate such sleazy establishments and have

such careless methods of publishing a book that very often the text of a work is so mutilated that it has a new, monstrous identity. However, says Mathews, horrible as these conditions are, they will soon pass, for "a thousand voices now slumber in our vales, amid our cities and along our hill-sides, that only await the genial hour to speak and to be heard," and that hour is near (16).

In Mathews' novels, *Big Abel and the Little Manhattan* (1845) and *Moneypenny, or, The Heart of the World* (1849), Mathews graphically describes the plight of American authors who labor under the unfair conditions he had attacked in his speech at the Dickens dinner. In *Big Abel,* the vignette showing the efforts of the poor scholar William to publish his book and to get a fair financial return represents the difficulties of far too many American writers. William already has had one book published; but it has brought him little reward, for Big Abel says of him, "he had a case in Court once, I recollect. It was all about a book, and the judge said it was a glorious thing to write a book; and that's all he got for it."[6] Such a situation, in which writers get "glory" and little else, will continue until a writer's work is regarded as legally his property.

Despite the misfortunes of his last book, William, after long labors, has completed another and is elated that he has thus succeeded in bringing into being "that little rounded Life which he had discerned lying in the midst of many things; that plan of a Book unborn, which might grow to beauty in his brain" (30). Adding to his happiness is the belief that the book will bring in enough money to enable him to marry his fiancée, Mary. Unfortunately, William's elation is cut short by the sordid realities of the American publishing business. Repeatedly, publication of his book is postponed as some new foreign work, for which American publishers do not have to pay royalties, is pirated by his publisher and brought out in its stead. Soon, William, despondent and fearful, spends his days looking out to sea, trembling "lest too happy speed . . . should bring some fatal ship to blight his hope; bearing from far lands some other book to take the place of his" (69).

Finally, after suffering innumerable disappointments and indignities, William sees his book published. The narrator exults, the book is "now gone forth (thank God!) to bless the world: . . . to bear a promise of his native land to every clime: to make this Home of his (for that it meant) grow bright and shine anew to all mankind" (77). Mathews obviously wants to please his readers by giving a happy ending to the sentimental vignette of William and Mary, but this ending is not a usual one in a nation plagued by predatory publishers and by the lack of an international copyright law.

A more typical situation, because of its hopelessness, is that of a serious young writer, George Eaglestone, which is described in *Moneypenny*. Eaglestone, forced by poverty to live in a tenement slum, attempts to create a literary work of real merit; and he barely survives while writing it by doing hack work for mercenary publishers. Mathews describes young Eaglestone's conversation with the "proprietor of a ladies magazine" who cares little for literature and "may be set down as a dealer in candles, lumber, calico, or hardware, or any of the everyday commodities." Indeed, he treats Eaglestone's work as he would a piece of dry-goods:

"I want a sonnet of about fourteen lines from you, Eaglestone. How much will you charge?"
"You paid me fifty cents for the last."
"That's too much—thirty-seven and a half cents is enough."
"Very well—just as you say."
"Where is it?"
"I have none written just now."
"Well, send it in as soon as you can."[7]

This patron leaves hurriedly to track down a two-volume novel which he hopes to get for twenty-five dollars or less, and Eaglestone puts aside his important work to grind out a sonnet.

III *The Literary Pirate*

The personages most responsible for keeping the lives of aspiring American writers like William and Eaglestone from being happy ones are the unethical publishers who practice literary piracy. Attacking these men in the article "John Smith, A Convicted Felon, Upon the Copyright," Mathews, assuming the persona of a habitual thief, pretends to attack the copyright policy which he has consistently advocated.[8] By doing so, he effects a caustic satire on those who oppose international copyright. As "John Smith," he claims it a heinous crime for an author who is little more than "a paltry blotter of paper, who seldom has a wife or children, because the ladies generally look on him as a fool or madman, [to] dare to ask . . . for pay, because [people] condescend to employ him to amuse a tedious hour." If the author must live, then, let him steal: "let us all steal and resolve society into its elements" (370). Smith declares that all want to fight crime, and he believes that the best means of doing so is to lift the various restrictions imposed by laws. Consequently, as long as the literary nationalists do not have their way—as long, then, as there is no international copyright—there will be no crime in literary piracy; and we will have successfully kept the national crime rate down (371). Smith, although a caricature, is merely based on a logical extension of the beliefs motivating the frequently amoral booksellers of Mathews' day.

In *The Career of Puffer Hopkins* (1842) Mathews presents an unsentimental, satiric sketch of literary piracy at work to show the conditions which keep deserving American authors poor, unpublished, and desperate. Mathews' creation, Mr. Piddleton Bloater, publisher of the *Mammoth Mug,* a newly established weekly, represents the American publishing establishment at its worst. Bloater is observed persuading a group of New York newsboys to sell his new paper to the exclusion of others that they have been hawking. He tells them that it "will be the completest paper ever published; eight feet square, honest measure; illustrated by the most splendid wood cuts, head-pieces, tail-pieces, and so forth, by the most celebrated artists." And, greatest news of all, he whispers the "astounding secret" that "Rumfusti, the Patriarch of Jerusalem, is employed to write an entirely original Continuous Tale for the *Mug.*" This last news impresses the newsboys: "if Rum-Buster out 'o Noah's ark writes for the first number," says one, "I'll cut in for a gross of number one; if I seed his Tale's name in big letters on the fences it 'ud give me confidence."[9]

The last point about which the newsboys have to be assured, however, is the most important one: "does the *Mug* go Captain Kidd, or the moral code?" In other words, does it pirate foreign material, thereby taking advantage of the lack of a copyright law? Bloater answers proudly: "Captain Kidd—decidedly. . . . We shall pirate all foreign tales regularly, and where we can purloin proof sheets shall publish in advance of the author himself; shall in all cases employ third-rate native writers at journeyman-cobbler's wages, and swear to their genius as a matter of business: shall reprint the old annuals and almanacs systematically as select extracts and facetiae" (138). The speaker for the newsboys, gratified, replies, "that'll do—that'll do. Set me down for the balance of the first edition: it'll be a first rate paper, and conducted on first rate principles" (138).

Bloater then makes one more point that is "to be distinctly and clearly understood. Whoever writes the chief article of the *Mug* is to be the great writer—the biggest penman that week." He mentions two universally detested writers and declares that, if they write for the *Mug,* each shall be boomed as "an angel in large caps" and as "a genius of the first water" (138). All the newsboys agree, knowing that such literary "puffing" is a highly profitable and therefore widely accepted practice. Obviously, when the publishing establishment is run by such men as Piddleton Bloater, serious American writers have little hope of success.

Mathews believed that the dishonest practices of the publishers taint the morality of society at large, and he emphasized this point in "An Appeal to American Authors and the American Press in Behalf of International Copyright" (1842). When a situation exists, such as that of American authors, in which large numbers of people "project but do not realize" and "sow but do not reap," all men suffer, for, he states, no "community is secure . . . where any law or fundamental right is systematically violated." From such a wrong an "atmosphere of pestilence" spreads, "in which all kindred rights moulder and decay. . . ."[10] A concrete instance of this "spreading pestilence" is the recent fire which destroyed the Harper and Brothers publishing establishment, a conflagration thought to be caused by a piratical publisher's effort to steal Harper's galley sheets of the new English novel, *Morley Ernstein.* It seems, then, that, when the morality of a country is tainted by such mean practices as the pirating of foreign books, it is a matter of course that immorality both proliferates and takes more vicious and violent forms (5).

Mathews attacks the principle on which piracy is based by declaring that, contrary to the greedy publishers' stated beliefs, a literary work is the legal property of the man who wrote it, just as much as the farmer's crop is his property. The publisher thinks, or declares that he does, that "the type, stitching, and paper are

THE BOOK! He forgets that when you buy a book, you do not buy the whole body of its thoughts in their entire breadth and construction" (8). For a publisher to appropriate the work of a man's mind and to sell it is just as much a theft as it would be for the author to steal the printed books from the publisher and sell them without giving him any return. Unfortunately, the publisher does not accept such arguments; he counters, instead, with the statement that he is actually performing a valuable function for the public in bringing good literature to it at extremely reasonable prices. Mathews, who considers this argument more specious than real, declares that "cheap and good are a pleasant partnership, but it does not happen that they always do business together." More often than not, the workmanship of the pirated books is shoddy; moreover, the book chosen for cheap publication is too often poorly written. Pushing this idea of cheapness to its extreme, Mathews declares that, if we were to use economy as our chief motivating force, we would "drive literature to the almanac, which can be afforded at a penny," and the era of the brown ballad would return "in all its primitive graces of an unclean sheet, a cloudy typography, and a style of thought and expression quite as pure and lucid." Truth and honesty, he asserts, are of more worth than "a reading public even as wide as the borders of the land" (13).

In speaking of the benefits that international copyright will bring to native literature and, hence, to the American public, Mathews scoffs at those who claim that advocates of copyright are unrealistic visionaries: "do I imagine then that an International Law will create great writers? Not at all." Under any law, writers of great genius "will struggle into light and cast before the world the thoughts with which their souls have been moved"; but the wide class of capable and honest, though not brilliant, writers would be aided by such a law. These men, who compose the body of a national literature, have been silenced too long by the existing inequitable situation; "it is these that need the constant stimulus, the genial inspiration (denied to them in any great measure by nature) of pay. It is shining gold, decry it as we may, that breeds the shining thought" (14–15). Mathews closes this essay by appealing to the press, asking it to aid its writing brethren, the authors, for in so doing, "that Union which, in politics and war, is strength, will prove in literature, as well, your champion and deliverer" (16).

IV *"Books Written by Free Men for Free Men"*

Continuing his appeal to the highest principles of his audience, Mathews, in the lecture "The Better Interests of the Country in Connection with International Copyright" (delivered at the New York Society Library on February 9, 1843) speaks of the important role literature plays in American life and of the multifarious dangers implicit in foreign books. He accurately describes Americans as a people who value education highly, and he sees this desire for education as making the United States a nation of readers. Therefore, it is of vital importance that this nation, which has no fixed standards of judgment, "read aright":

Having no central standards of opinion, no fixed classes as examples and guides, her mind is the result of a constant intercommunication of part with part, section with section, through the press. The general sum of her reading represents and controls her thoughts, her habits and her government. Her institutions modeled originally on the necessities of her situation in place, time and progress of opinion, must be sustained by a literature . . . assimilating with these, or be modified by another literature which is too rigid to coalesce, and strong enough to break in pieces and appropriate to itself whatever it approaches.[11]

This other dangerous literature is, of course, British literature, which often is implicitly a spokesman for a nondemocratic society, flooding America with its alien principles.[12]

Mathews reiterates that, instead of supporting publishers who pirate foreign books and, in effect, suppressing native works, the American public must have a moral commitment to sustain home authors; for only they can articulate American values and needs and lead citizen readers to accomplish the necessary actions to improve the nation. Again Mathews declares that literary works are the property of their creators, but he attempts this time to prove it on a philosophical plane. He believes it is obvious that we all do not share one universal mind, and he claims that those who believe such nonsense are dangerous in that "this new dream of the universal commonness of soul and thought would fill the universe with God and void it of his creatures." Thoughts make men individuals, and each man's thoughts are his own. Thus, whatever is created by a man's mind is uniquely his; to take it from him is to violate his individuality and, in fact, his property (9).

However, the flood of foreign literature into America violates individuality in an even more subtle manner by forcing American writers into imitativeness. Not being able to find a market for original, peculiarly American works, they try to compete with popular English imports by slavishly imitating them. This practice makes for an effete, bastardized literature which is not an expression of America and has little to say to Americans: "One gentleman . . . furnishes a most moving and pathetic tale of a ribband or a hair-veil, another, a light and airy poem of sentiment about nothing; and, another, the delightful history of Arthur Melton, and all his agreeably commonplace love passages with the charming young heroine, Helen Edgecomb" (20). Instead of such a worthless literature, Mathews envisions what American literature should have developed into and what it still might be if international copyright were passed. At first, it certainly would not be a "mature, harmonious, complete literature"; but it would consist of words "at least spontaneous in their growth, and akin, in some measure, to the life of man in a world full of suggestive newness both to eye and spirit." Its books would be "rugged as the mountains and cataracts among which they were produced." They would have "something of a lusty strength" and a "certain grandeur of thought, a wild, barbaric splendor." In such a nation as America, "where the free spirit lifts its head and speaks what it will," the native literature, "should have something more to say" (22).

Such a virile, native literature would, in time, be engendered by a copyright agreement. A legitimate, reputable class of publishers would develop; the practice of "puffing" worthless foreign books would end; and American criticism would assume a nobler role—that of setting high standards, principles, and guidelines for American authors. Consequently, there would be a greater productiveness in literature, both numerically and qualitatively. This literature would have repercussions in Europe as well; for English writers, finding a profitable market for their books in the United States, might actually write with an eye to American ideas and their new, democratic tone might work a significant change in England and the rest of Europe (28).

An America united and given a sense of purpose through the establishment of a national literature might play an important role in the course of world history. In "Americanism," an address delivered in 1845 before the Eucleian Society of New York University, Mathews speaks of the responsibility that Americans have to the rest of the world and to posterity: "We, it so happens, form the first generation of Americans reared, from infancy to manhood—along the whole line of our lives, minute by minute, year by year—in the doctrine and under the discipline of Republican Truth. . . . The task our fathers had to do, they did well; but it was not our task. . . . Our duty and our destiny is another from theirs."[13] To Mathews, America's twenty million people represent twenty million sovereign republics—each in its own right—and thus each becomes a fearful force for good or evil: "you and others akin to you, are to take a great part in supplying motives to these millions of sovereign energies, in giving impulse to the spirit and a language to the voice of yet mightier millions that draw near" (19).

A distinctly American literature could provide this kind of inspiration through describing Americans and their way of life. This nationality, he says, will not be that "declaimed in taverns, ranted of in Congress, or made the occasion of boasting and self-laudation or public anniversaries." Nor will it "grow cross-eyed with straining its vision on models, three thousand miles away, while it makes a show of busying itself with a subject spread on the desk before it" (20). Mathews says that the time has come when Americans will no longer be moved either by the empty bombastic rhetoric of jingoistic know-nothings or by the "tinkling rhymers and sketchers with sparrow's quills" who see nothing but England (21). Instead, Americans demand a literature built "on a base of sure good sense, and embracing in a catholic spirit all that is good and of good influence in all the world: drawing it home to their native land in a true nationality, and returning it again to the world that gave it, to bless, and cheer and purify all mankind" (23). So pressing is the issue, Mathews believes, that America must "have Home-Thoughts" or, spiritually speaking, it will "cease to live" (27–28). In fact, an American literature is what the world demands because it is "revolutionizing slowly under the influence of our example" (29). But Americans also need this kind of literature "more and more, to keep us true to our own ideal—for ourselves. Books written by Free Men for Free Men" (29–30).

Such a literature, constantly recalling Americans to the high purposes with which the nation was founded, would inspire them to work unceasingly to make their country's life a better one: "She cannot like others pause, and falter, and look back. Everyday she must make some progress, or confess herself laggard and treacherous. Everyday she must fix her eye upon some new point to be reached—must lay her hand upon some evil, in the social system, to be plucked away—must brighten and raise up some truth. . . . Everyday she must . . . repeat to herself line by line, principle by principle, the mighty creed to which she is sworn" (33).

Less high-minded, but perhaps more effective, potentially, is the appeal to practicality and jingoism made by Mathews, William Cullen Bryant, and Francis L. Hawks, as spokesmen for the American Copyright Club in "An Address to the People of the United States in Behalf of the American Copyright Club" (1843). While these American writers reiterate many of the moral arguments for copyright, they also try to show the businessmen-publishers that its passage would make good sense financially, for it would aid reputable publishing houses by getting rid of fly-by-night affairs. Furthermore, they try to convince vote-conscious congressmen that the national pride demands a native literature and that such a literature must be protected from insidious foreign subversion—"will the pamphlet carry the day where the soldiers fell back?"[14] Since a worldwide conflict for the minds of men is going on between England and America, the challenge is theirs: "Now it lies with you, in some measure, to determine whether your best and manliest spirits shall be sent to the field: whether all, in truth, of every order, rank and power, shall enter for the cause without bar or shackle, free as the general air, to a fair encounter" (17). Unfortunately, even such a well-conceived appeal failed to secure the passage of the copyright bill.

In essays, speeches, and fiction, Cornelius Mathews continually maintained that, for a nation to flourish spiritually and intellectually as well as materially, it must have a literature that articulated its own ideals and goals. Such a literature would never develop, he believed, until the influx of foreign books into America was stopped and until American writers were, consequently, encouraged to turn to home subjects. International copyright finally was adopted in 1891, long after a distinctly American literature was well established. However, it seems that the efforts of Mathews and men like him, such as William Dean Howells and others later in the century,

went a long way toward creating at atmosphere in which American
literary themes and expression could evolve. Moreover, copyright
itself, while no longer necessary to protect a struggling American
literature, was still an effective means of gaining writers more
equitable treatment. Thus, both artistically and commercially,
Mathews' long and often unpopular efforts were vindicated.

CHAPTER 3

Mathews' Use of Historical Resources

I *The Heroic Landscape*

CORNELIUS Mathews realized that if American writers were to create a distinctly American literature, rather than continue slavishly following their European counterparts, they had to be made to see that American traditions, people, and physical landscape provided material for literary endeavor. Consequently, in his own work Mathews tried to show that a writer did not have to journey to Europe for "inspiration" or, in lieu of this pilgrimage, look longingly over the water, lamenting that all the tradition, all the epic grandeur, and all the beauty were somehow there. Like Timothy Dwight and Joel Barlow at the end of the eighteenth century, Mathews attempted to use the American past in order to create works of an "epic" scope; and he hoped thus to prove to his contemporaries that their own land was one rich with its distinct kind of tradition and grandeur.

In both *Behemoth; A Legend of the Mound-builders* (1839) and *Wakondah; The Master of Life* (1841) Mathews tried to create national epics[1] that would provide his countrymen with a native, heroic mythology; and he went back to the prehistorical society of the Mound-builders and to the legends of the American Indian to do so. Similarly, in *Big Abel and the Little Manhattan* (1845)—an attempt to capture the magnificent, expansive energy of the American metropolis, New York City—an Indian, Lankey Fogle, serves as a visible link to the heroic American past (as does the white man, Big Abel, a descendant of Henry Hudson). In these works, as well as in *Chanticleer* (1850) and in *Witchcraft* (1846), which, although not of epic intentions, glorify the American past, a major continuing theme is that Americans do, in fact, have a past that permeates the landscape of the present and ennobles both it and those who inhabit it. This past is, then, so important that American writers must deal with it in their work.

II   Behemoth

In contemptuously dismissing *Behemoth,* Perry Miller calls it "about as ridiculous a fanfaronade as the age produced."[2] Perhaps it is, largely, an ineffective work as Miller believes; but though *Behemoth* has its shortcomings, the concept behind it makes it a book which ought not to be ignored. Indeed, Mathews himself, in a letter to Evert Duyckinck, spoke of *Behemoth* "as an Experiment of the boldest and most hazardous kind."[3] In his preface Mathews states that his "main design was to make those gigantic relics, which are found scattered throughout this country, subservient to purposes of the imagination" which would imbue them with their rightful grandeur by re-creating the heroic past of which they are the only remains. Furthermore, he speaks of the vastness and beauty of the American landscape and emphasizes that stories of the interaction of men and such an environment should be enough to provide a wealth of subjects for any true artist. Indeed, few topics are more intrinsically striking than that of man's trying to make a place for himself in nature. Therefore, no American has to go to Europe to contemplate ruins and monuments to conjure up images of a heroic past; the American scene has more than enough for him.[4]

That Mathews is consciously attempting to create an epic of the American scene is apparent from the first in *Behemoth.* The novel opens with a majestic description of craggy peaks and a "gigantic shape"—a landscape of heroic proportions: "Upon the summit of a mountain which beetled in the remote west over the dwellings and defences of a race long since vanished, stood, at the close of a midsummer's day, a gigantic shape whose vastness darkened the whole vale beneath. The sunset purpled the mountain-top, and crimsoned with its deep, gorgeous tints the broad occident, and as the huge figure leaned against it, it seemed like a mighty image cut from the solid peak itself, and framed against the sky" (1). This landscape does not dwarf its inhabitants, for they, in proportion, are a race of heroes who "accomplished a career in the West, corresponding, though less magnificent and imposing, with that which the Greeks and Romans accomplished in what is styled by courtesy the Old World. The hour has been when our own West was thronged with Empires" (2).

Our first view of the Mound-builders finds them performing their daily rites of worship before their sun-god. However, on this day, as they look reverently toward the setting sun, they see, blotting it out, the dark, ominous shape of a gigantic mastodon; it first seems to them to be a monster exhibited by the gods of evil in order to astonish and awe them. Mathews likens the behemoth to a dark force of nature, more like a tornado or an earthquake than an animate being; it seems an "awful ridge, rolling like a billow" or an island wracked by some convulsion of nature (19). As it advances, the forest trembles, and even its fiercest animal inhabitants skulk away. The description of a beast which frightens even the wolf and the panther makes the behemoth seem larger than life, a more-than-natural force to be contended with by a race of heroes against a backdrop of grandiose proportions.

From this account of the basic situation in *Behemoth,* we see that many of the usual elements of the epic genre are present. The setting provides the sense of spaciousness and magnitude associated with the epic, for it encompasses the Rocky Mountains and the great American plains, whose epic possibilities are increased by Mathews' unconventional treatment of them. According to the conventional view, the West was a "tenantless and houseless desert," wild and unpeopled, except for bands of straggling Indians or an occasional herd of buffalo. But, according to Mathews, the vast prairies were heavily populated with "countless" cities whose majestic mounds and towers of granite and marble rose to heights which seemed to rival those attained by the neighboring mountain peaks (80–81).[5] This combination of untamed nature and flourishing civilization adds to the inherent drama of Mathews' plot by providing a strong visual contrast between the environment man has constructed for himself and the natural world with which he must still contend. Also, it anticipates for us, symbolically, the larger conflict to come (one dealt with by Mathews in subsequent work) as the latter-day Americans, successors to the Mound-builders, advance across a rugged, unyielding continent.

In keeping with such a setting, we find, as in all epics, a brave people attempting to carry out valiant actions on which hinges the survival of their whole society. The heroic code by which this nation lives is illustrated by Mathews through his description of its military burial rites. At some length, he tells of how those who have died in battle are interred with ritualistic martial ceremony, their bodies swathed in the finest clothing, their weapons at their right hand, and at their sides mirrors "in which they were wont to look for the reflection of their own martial features when set for the stern service of war" (15).

Again as in most epics, the story is centered on one heroic figure whose deeds and words, in great part, epitomize the actions and desires of the whole nation. In *Behemoth* this communal leader is Bokulla, the chief, who in his best moments—those when he ventures out alone to attack the giant mastodon—seems patterned after Beowulf in his battles against Grendel and Grendel's dam. Bokulla's greatness is apparent in Mathews' first description of him: he is a man of "singular and prompt courage, of great earnestness of purpose and energy of character; yet modest and unobtrusive" (12). His people depend on him: "when all eyes were turned towards him as the last star of hope, he sprang with alacrity to the front, prepared to match the emergency" with courage and ability. Moreover, he is no rash glory-hound, but "a philosopher no less than a soldier" (12).

This description is borne out by Bokulla's demeanor through the rest of the work, as it is the courageous Bokulla around whom his people rally. Thus, after the mastodon makes his first appearance, spreading destruction and death, and the Mound-builders lose heart, their spirit broken by the magnitude of the beast's havoc, Bokulla endeavors to encourage them. Only he is able to put their problem in a larger perspective—to see it as more than just a battle against an overpowering beast. Rather, he tells his people, appealing to their sense of dignity, that the struggle is between man, attempting to maintain his heroic destiny, and the brute, stupid forces of nature: "is man, who thus outlasted seas, and stars, and mountains, to be crushed at last by mere brutal enginery and corporal strength[?]" As Bokulla harangues them in terms of national pride, he tells the Mound-builders that their traditions and values will become worthless and their courageous forebears will be dishonored if they allow the mastodon to defeat them. Bokulla is, therefore, his people's communal spokesman, as well as their military leader, who articulates their traditions, aims, and values.

After responding to Bokulla's words, the Mound-builders prepare an offensive against the mastodon, a campaign for what

Mathews calls "the redemption of a people." In this effort the Mound-builders have developed a powerful arsenal of various "battle-engines" and of "vast bows and poisoned shafts, with which, if such thing might be, to pierce him [Behemoth] in some vulnerable point, or at least to gall him sorely and drive him at a distance" (34). In Mathews' detailed picture of each element of the titanic struggle to come, he is not merely attempting to achieve verisimilitude; instead, he provides a vivid sense of these people and their way of life. This effort is necessary in creating an epic; and seven years later, Herman Melville made a similar attempt, but with greater effectiveness, in "Cetology" in *Moby Dick*.

As the army of Mound-builders starts out, amid the plaudits of their countrymen, to find and destroy Behemoth, a note of foreboding is sounded by an old man and his wife who hold little hope for Bokulla's expedition because they remember that in time long past the "fellow of this vast Brute (perchance this living one himself)" had badly defeated a brave army of Mound-builders (39). The old couple's linking of this beast with one which had devastated their fathers provides Behemoth with an aura of timelessness, thereby increasing the drama and magnitude of the struggle that confronts the Mound-builders. Moreover, the prophecy of doom proves accurate; the mighty army is crushed, and its remnants are put to rout by the rampaging monster. In fact, the Mound-builders, thrown into a state of hysterical paralysis merely at the sight of Behemoth, are defeated before the battle even begins. They come upon him while he swims in the ocean:

> The giant beast seemed to be sporting with the ocean. For a moment he plunged into it, and swimming out a league with his head and lithe proboscis reared above the waters, spouted forth a sea of bright fluid toward the sky, ascending to the very cloud, which returning, brightened into innumerable rainbows, large and small, and spanned the ocean. Again he cast his huge bulk along the main, and lay "floating many a rood" in the soft middle sun, basking in its ray and presenting in the grandeur and vastness of his repose, a monumental image of Eternal Quiet. Bronze nor marble have ever been wrought into sculpture as grand and sublime as the motionless shape of that mighty Brute resting on the sea. (52–53)

In this passage Mathews effectively emphasizes the grandeur of the giant mastodon; and, as Perry Miller and Curtis Dahl point out, such a description is not unlike Melville's picture of the epic whale

Moby Dick.[6] Again, like Moby Dick, something strange and enigmatic exists in Behemoth's physical appearance; something lurks
behind the visage, some universal meaning, perhaps, not readily per-
ceivable to man. The behemoth seems to transcend this world, but
he also appears as inextricably part of the firmament which "rests
upon his wide shoulders as a mantle." Indeed, he comes "between
them and heaven," filling the "whole circuit of the sky"; but he
turns toward them a face which looks as if it has been cut from stone,
with features "large as those of the Egyptian Sphinx" (55), whose
aura of mystery he presumably shares. Contemplating this enigma
of massive violence, the army is spiritually defeated from the first.

With the army's defeat, the responsibility for saving the nation
falls to its leader, Bokulla. While the Mound-builders now find the
world dreary and evil and languish in depression, Bokulla, isolated
by his continued resolve, works at restoring their morale; but it
becomes increasingly apparent that he alone will have to rid the
land of the terror. Realizing this fact, he goes into the wilderness to
observe Behemoth's habits and, thus, perhaps, find some way of
destroying him. This journey into the wilds throws the chief of the
Mound-builders into a closer conjunction with nature, thus en-
larging him and making him seem a fitter adversary for the giant
mastodon. On his lonely hunt Bokulla reaffirms his belief in man's
ability to conquer the destructive forces of nature, for he sees the
earth and its creatures as given to man for his dominion (82).

Knowing that the wilderness must be met on its own terms,
Bokulla takes no food with him, casting himself on nature "to be
received and sustained by her as a worthy child, or to perish as an
alien and outcast on her bosom" (83). Nature responds to this
trust by showing Bokulla its benevolent aspects. He feels, gathering around him, strange stirrings and emotions, conjured up by
the woodland, telling him that he is not alone. He declares, "immortal powers and faculties! In these retired and natural chambers,
I know you as the internal and silent agencies which are to guide
and sustain me through this hardy and venturous pilgrimage"
(85). Thus, Bokulla, himself, seems increasingly to become a force
of nature. Adding to his heroic proportions and to the magnitude
of his quest is Bokulla's dream in which the mountains are battered
and rocked by violent winds, "While in their midst one mighty
Figure, neither of man nor of angel, stood chained, and, in a

deep and fearful voice, cried to the heavens for succor" (93). Bokulla has, therefore, the archetypal role of savior of the people, the role of a Prometheus.

Because we recognize the transcendent importance of Bokulla's mission, as well as characteristics of the epic, we are not surprised when Bokulla is aided by supernatural intervention. When he discovers the canyon in which the mastodon usually dwells, he evolves a plan to destroy the monster; but only divine aid enables him to live to put his plan into action. After discovering Behemoth's dwelling place, Bokulla, lost and starving, wanders the desert tormented by hunger and anguish. Nature, though, saves him by sending a hawk, which Bokulla spies while it carries its prey. He pursues it, hoping it will somehow drop its quarry, enabling him to make a meal. The pursuit, becoming almost obsessive on Bokulla's part, stretches across miles of barren desert. Finally, faint with fatigue and hunger, Bokulla is saved by coming upon and capturing a wild, jet-black horse. Now, astride this romantic-looking steed, Bokulla continues his race after the hawk; finally, without being aware of his progress, he finds himself led home.

The overwhelming effects of Bokulla's experiences in the wilderness are evidenced by his countrymen's inability to recognize him. Frightened by Bokulla's haggard, wild appearance and by the storming, black charger, one Mound-builder shouts that Bokulla is "a fiend of the prairie, he that rambles up and down the big meadow, blowing his horn and who calls the wolves and goblins together when a carcass is thrown out or a traveller perishes" (101).

On returning, Bokulla finds the Mound-builders still demoralized, still without the will to resist. The adverse effect that Behemoth has had on their state of mind is vividly portrayed by the deathbed ramblings of one who has been mortally wounded by the monster and now breaks into wild invective, deliriously imagining it before him: "This huge bully: this fleshy continent: this vagabond traveller: this beast-mountain: this tornado in leather: this bristly goblin ... this Empire of bones and sinew: this monstrous government on legs: this Tyrant with a tail ... this walking abomination: this enormous Discord sounding in base" (106–7). These vitriolic epithets provide additional insight into the enormity of the mastodon's impact on the nation. Furthermore, they emphasize once more just how huge and all-encompassing this beast seems to be:

finally, they emphasize the essential difference between the hero-leader Bokulla and the average man. Bokulla does not rail and lament; instead, he goes out and, with calm fortitude, attempts to achieve.

Bokulla leads a group of warriors to Behemoth's valley and goads them into a courageous frame of mind before telling them of his plan. First, many are timid, but Bokulla's scornful suggestions of "an embassy to the brute on bended knee," in which they might appeal to him as worshipers and offer to make him their national idol, prompt them to react courageously, and they vow to die, if need be, with "the heavens themselves and the inexorable stars [as] witnesses of [their] struggle" (117). Bokulla's plan, to beguile Behemoth with music, and, meanwhile, wall up the single entrance into his canyon, is successful. The mastodon is left to face death by starvation, and his death throes are commensurate with his enormous bulk and power:

Around and around the firm Colosseum which enclosed him, he rushed maddened, bellowing and foaming.
    At times, in his fury, he pushed up the almost perpendicular sides of the mountains and recoiled, bringing with him shattered fragments of rock and large masses of earth, with fearful force and swiftness. Around and around he again galloped and trampled, shaking the very mountains with his ponderous motions, and filling their whole circuit with his terrible howlings and cries. (123)

The allusion to the Colosseum is Mathews' not-so-subtle reminder that his tale is just as grand and heroic as any that derives from the ancient world. Also, as in the case of the world's great epics, the events described in *Behemoth* are not readily forgotten because, although the mastodon and its hunters are gone, their presence, through various artifacts found in the American West, lingers on to evoke a misty but noble past.

Throughout Mathews' depiction of the struggle between Behemoth and the Mound-builders, he makes use of various literary devices which envelop the events with an atmosphere of majesty and glory. These devices include the various image patterns which he sets up and the diction and rhythms of his prose style. First, we note continual visual references to gigantic objects in nature, providing images of "craggy" mountain peaks, "endless" horizons, "surging" rivers, wide, barren deserts, the planets, and the heavens. The largeness of nature is matched by its violence, which is delineated by numerous images of beasts of prey, avalanches, earthquakes, raging storms, and burning suns. These two patterns of imagery unite to form a picture of a world that is both awesome in size and frightening in its violence; and the grandeur of this world makes the people inhabiting it also seem grand and important.

This effect is further conveyed through Mathews' prose style, which in *Behemoth* is a pretentious one full of inflated diction and oppressively heavy rhythms. His description of the flow of years and its effect on the Mound-builders is typical: "Over that Archipelago of nations the Dead Sea of Time has swept obliviously, and subsiding, hath left their graves only the greener for a new people in the present age to build their homes thereon" (2). Similarly, Mathews uses little dialogue, not wanting to let the readers get too close to the Mound-builders and view them as actual people rather than as a race of heroes. The few passages of dialogue in *Behemoth* are, for the most part, speeches by Bokulla, which are characterized by Mathews' effort to fashion a soaring rhetoric in keeping with the stature of the speaker, as when Bokulla describes the contempt their dead ancestors would feel for the demoralized Mound-builders:

Are these men, that creep along the earth, like the pale shadows of Autumn, Mound-builders and children of our loins? What hath affrighted them? Look to the mountains, and lo! an inferior creature, one of the servants and hirelings of man, hath the mastery. Arouse! Arouse! our sons! Place in our old, death-withered hands the swords we once wielded—crown us with our familiar helms and we will wage the battle for you. Victory to the builders of the mounds! victory to the lords and masters of the earth! should be our cry of onset and triumph! (31)

Often such speeches devolve into tin-plated bombast. However, the heroic effect, although perhaps a bit turgid, is still conveyed.

Behemoth celebrates the American past and attempts to glorify it in order to make contemporary Americans aware that their land has a history as ancient and noble as any in Europe. In an afterword, Mathews, speaking of America's past and future, declares that, as time passes and our nation becomes one of the leaders of the world, we will inevitably feel a strong sense of kinship with the "unrecorded race that has departed like a shadow, from the glorious and magnificent West" (132).

III   *The Passing of Old Masters*

Mathews' long, narrative poem, *Wakondah; The Master of Life,* deals with a more recent period in American history than does *Behemoth;* for he laments the passing of the Indian and his way of life from the American scene. A tradition of native independence and heroism has departed; in its place, we find the white Americans' crass materialism and sense of cultural inferiority. In *Wakondah,* as in *Behemoth,* Mathews endeavors to imbue this lost tradition with epic qualities. However, instead of emphasizing the heroic attributes of a nation which is trying to maintain itself against an often hostile environment, as he did in *Behemoth,* Mathews focuses on a man-god's transcendent communion with nature.

As a headnote to *Wakondah,* Mathews uses a passage from Washington Irving's *Astoria,* in which Irving speaks of the religious veneration with which the Indians regard the Rocky Mountains. They call the range "The Crest of the World" and believe that Wakondah, or "The Master of Life" as they designate the Supreme Being, inhabits its peaks. Mathews presents this Supreme Being, or Wakondah, as an epitome and apotheosis of the Indian warrior; therefore Wakondah represents both man and God.

Like the Titans in Keats's "Hyperion," Wakondah feels his powers to be in decline since he no longer achieves the close union with nature which gave him control over its forces. When he attempts to assert once more his dominion over them by calling the forests to tremble and the cataracts to resound as a pledge of their fealty to him, they fail to respond:

> The woods are deaf and will not be aroused—
>   The mountains are asleep, they hear him not,
>   Nor from deep-founded silence can be wrought,
> Tho' herded bison on their steeps have browsed:
> Beneath their banks in darksome stillness housed
>   The rivers loiter like a calm-bound sea;
>   In anchored nuptials to dumb apathy
> Cliff, wilderness and solitude are spoused.[7]

The picture of cliffs, cataracts, and crags and the auditory imagery of "howling winds" and "sullen roars" combine to evoke a world of grandeur and tremendous violence—a world soon to be displaced by a less heroic, more insidiously and subtly violent one.

The Wakondah, symbolic representation of the old way of life, which is failing just as he is, speaks of the days when he still maintained sway over the American continent. In his speech Mathews idealizes these lost days, for he hopes to make his readers see that something valuable has vanished and been forgotten:

> My spirit stretched itself from East to West,
> With a winged terror or a mighty joy;
> And, when his matchless bow-shafts would annoy,
> I urged the dark red hunter in his quest
> Of pard or panther with a gloomy zest,
> And while through darkling woods they swiftly fare—
> Two seeming creatures of the oak-shadowed air,
> I sped the game and fired the follower's breast. (14)

Such days are over, as this hero is too large to survive in the new world established by white settlers. Grandiose proportions must be cut down to size for a people who are Lilliputian spiritually. The Wakondah is told of his destiny—the power will crumble from his arm, and glory shall soon decline from his brow. The time is fast coming when the sun shall cease to shine upon him because he must make way for a new controlling force, "a glorious white and shining deity./Upon our strength his deep blue eye he bends,/With threatenings full of thought and steadfast ends" (15).

The Wakondah berates the white man for being a "nation queller," a "slaughterer of tribes" who thinks nothing of crushing a people and their culture, while despoiling their ancestral home (16). He envisions, accurately, the destruction and havoc that the white man will bring:

> At every step old shadows fly aloof,
> While on and on he bounds with strength enough
> To master valley, hill and echoing plain—
> Cheered by the outcry of a savage train
> Of white-browed hunters armed in deadly proof. (17)

He declares, however, that the day will come when "vengeance [will] bid the sons of men—Prepare!" On that day the land and its red inhabitants will take their revenge on the white despoiler (18).

The poet, speaking as an off-stage narrator, while agreeing with the general tenor of Wakondah's attack on the white man's society, denies that the newcomers will have to face a catastrophic Armageddon. He envisions, instead, a glorious future, a time when present problems will be long-since ameliorated, for he knows that Heaven has a great destiny in store for America and will pardon the white man his transgressions. Thus, the time will come when the boundaries of our nation will extend "from loud Atlantic unto Oregon" in an "orb of power" which shall never be yielded up and which shall serve forever as "a home and fortress to the free" (19). The vision of "manifest destiny" is in keeping with the poet's belief that it is not the white man alone who is driving out the Wakondah and the world he represents; the white man in America is merely the function of a larger design which runs the world, a destiny which cannot be gainsaid.

The poem ends on the note of affirmation sounded by the narrator. Although the Wakondah is destroyed as an actual entity, and his way of life is fast vanishing from the scene, still the spirit and world view of which he was a manifestation hover around America, and "still will have a tongue/Ere yet the winds have wafted them along/To endless silence" (24). The potential for heroism and a life of national nobility exists; all Americans need is a consciousness of it and an awareness of the possibilities of its attainment.

Among those uninspired by Mathews' efforts in *Wakondah* was Edgar Allan Poe, who in the February, 1842, number of *Graham's Magazine* reviewed the poem in great detail.[8] Poe declares: "if we mention it at all, we are *forced* to employ the language of that region where, as Addison has it, 'they sell the best fish and speak the plainest English.' Wakondah, then from beginning to end is trash" (26). Apart from some minor exceptions, Poe says "it has *no* merit whatever" (27). In general, he sees the poem as a compendium of bombastic rigmarole pieced together by the "most rhetorical, not to say the most miscellaneous orations we ever remember to have listened to outside of an Arkansas House of Delegates" (28).

After scoffing at the overall scheme of the poem, Poe enumerates the many errors in Mathews' slipshod poetic technique. He finds fault with Mathews for errors of diction, such as using the word "might" too often and using "utters forth" instead of "utters." More flagrant, though, are errors of perception: "The moon is described as 'ascending,' and its 'motion' is referred to, while we have the standing figure continuously intercepting its light. That the orb would soon pass from behind the figure, is a physical fact which the purpose of the poet required to be left out of sight, and which scarcely any other language than that which he has actually employed would have succeeded in forcing upon the reader's attention" (29). Similarly, Poe objects to Mathews' description of Wakondah's command to the rivers: "He now speaks to the night-shadowed Rivers, and commands them to lift their dusky hands, and clap them harshly *with a sullen roar*—and as *roaring* with one's *hands* is not the easiest matter in the world, we can only conclude that the Rivers here reluctantly disobeyed the injunction" (32). Finally, Poe attacks Mathews' prosody, finding it "droll," "*very* odd," and one in which "the rhythm demands an accent on impossible syllables" (36).

Undoubtedly, Poe's criticism of *Wakondah* is accurate; the poem is badly written. However, it is important to remember that a major reason for its sloppiness is that Mathews was wrestling with conceptions which were too large for his abilities. It would not have been too difficult for Mathews to create an unassuming, sentimental little lyric like Nathaniel Parker Willis' "Unseen Spirits," which Poe much admired; but Mathews sought something greater, as the tenor of the errors Poe points out in *Wakondah* indicates. Inflated diction is merely a heavy-handed attempt to magnify the importance of the subject matter; therefore, words like "might" are repeated indiscriminately, and swelling redundancies such as "utters forth" are substituted for the adequate "utters." For like reasons, huge figures blot out the moon, and the rivers sound "sullen roars." A writer's large conceptions, then, may often lead him to disregard the conventions of his craft; and, unless he has talent, the results can be ludicrous—as they frequently are in *Wakondah*. But Mathews' failure presages the successes of others like Walt Whitman who, with greater concepts and greater talent, broke more rules while adding something to the national spirit.

IV   *America in Transition*

From the heroic world of *Wakondah,* Mathews turned to the more prosaic society of his own time in his next attempt to write a distinctly American work with epical overtones, *Big Abel and the Little Manhattan.* Although this short novel describes a modern society in which characters of epic dimensions are out of place, Mathews endeavors, at the same time, to create an epic of the present world, one built on what is rather than what was. Thus, this work both attacks and glorifies contemporary American life: while criticizing the shabby and the banal, it extolls and idealizes the romantic and the vital.

Big Abel and the Little Manhattan are down-and-out New York City vagabonds who are outstanding in only one respect—Big Abel, whose full name is Abel Henry Hudson, is a direct descendant of the famous explorer; and Little Manhattan, Lankey Fogle, is the sole remainder of what had been a great tribe of Indians and a descendant of the chief who sold Manhattan to the Dutch. Therefore, these men, although fallen on bad times themselves, are visible reminders of an epic past. As representatives of the primitive inhabitants and the first immigrants, they have gone to court to claim title to Manhattan Island. Now, somehow persuaded that their claim is won, they walk through the city, apportioning it between them. Big Abel chooses for himself the civilized aspects of urban life—banks, office buildings, shops, and vehicles, the prison, and City Hall; but the Little Manhattan chooses the sites of old Indian camping grounds and tracts of woodland and park that are, as yet, unsullied by the city.

From this account of the story of the two friends, it is obvious that *Big Abel and the Little Manhattan* does not have much of a plot; but it is also apparent that an involved, carefully developed plot is not needed for Mathews' purposes. Typically, he is concerned less with specific events than with the conceptions behind them. Consequently, Big Abel and the Little Manhattan are not so important in themselves as in what they represent: two diametrically opposed world views, one primitive, yearning, wild; the other modern, "progressive," civilized. In the reactions of each character, as he observes various examples of New York City life, the reader is able to perceive these opposing world views, each of which Mathews idealizes throughout the story as grand and romantic. New York City itself, then, despite the prosaic, often ugly, tenor of its life, serves as the focal point of their perceptions, and, by its very largeness, aids in Mathews' efforts to imbue these perceptions with epic overtones. Therefore, Mathews does not need a carefully constructed, eventful plot; the episodic wandering and commentary which he uses is best suited to his aims.

Thus, it is Mathews' overall vision of American life which concerns us here, not the story itself. While overemphasizing, perhaps, the clumsiness of *Big Abel,* Perry Miller does grant that its shortcomings attest to the largeness of Mathews' attempt, which touches upon that "immense topic in modern literature," the "apocalyptic vision of the city."[9] Mathews' scope is even larger than this, however, for he tends to see the city as a symbolic representation of American life as a whole; and, ultimately, this novel is nothing less than an allegory with epical overtones describing the two great opposing forces—the kinship with a heroic past and the commitments to an essentially commercial present—which constitute the American psyche.

In order to emphasize from the first that even a commercial center like New York City, as well as the American wilderness, has an aura of the grandiose and romantic about it, Mathews opens his tale with a description of a great Shot-Tower which dominates the surrounding scene and which is soon to serve as the meeting place for a mysterious assignation between Big Abel and Lankey. The "great, white tower" rises "ghostlike" and holds "all the neighborhood in subjection to its repose and supernatural port." Indeed, it is "the ghost of New York, gone into the suburbs to meditate on the wickedness of mankind, and haunt the Big City," filling its dreams with visions of war and carnage from the past.[10]

On his way to the Shot-Tower, Lankey is introduced to the reader. He combines indigence and an almost supernatural grandeur, for when the sun is low in the sky, at its setting, its rays penetrate the holes in his clothing, "passing in at an elbow or coming out at the hand, or piercing him through from back to breast" and thus lighting him "with a sort of dim splendor" (3). Undoubtedly, Lankey is in a state of decline; the man himself is not impressive. However, the atmosphere of glory in which he moves is derived from the fact that he is the last vestige of a race of heroes, thereby making his present quest impressive. Essentially, his attempt to assert ownership of half of New York City symbolizes an older way of life trying to retain its foothold in the New World. This significance is revealed in the cryptic comment of a stranger who intercepts Lankey on his way to the Shot-Tower and who asserts that whether or not "the hopes of mankind are to be blighted" depends on the course that Lankey adopts after his meeting at the tower (6–7).

Unlike Lankey, Big Abel, although not extremely well off, does seem to be flourishing, for his tall, "goodly figure" is clothed in a new hat, bright new coat with brass buttons, and boots that still have the "pleasant creak" that says they have just left the shop. Manifestly a creature of this modern world, he stands "square upon the ground" (9). Although he has a heroic heritage, as does Lankey, his tradition is not a dying one; it is growing. Throughout the work, Big Abel becomes identified with the growing might and manifest destiny of the United States. An idealized version of the new American, he is aware of his heritage and looks with confidence to the future; and his portrait is not unlike the picture Whitman was to draw ten years later of the American democrat.

As the two men wander the city together, Lankey choosing for himself spots with Indian memories and Abel choosing modern areas and objects of the white man's world, Mathews emphasizes the differences between their two outlooks. Lankey, saddened and wistful, claims an old Indian burial ground; and, in doing so, he has a vision of the past when dusky men bore to "grassy hillocks there, a warrior with his bow, a maiden in her long black tress, a prophet in his cunning robe" and laid them in the earth; and, though the men went away for a time, they always came again, and still again, and never forgot their kinship with those who lay there, until they joined them (25). Big Abel, on the other hand, sees nothing but a waste-ground with a few idle trees and some old flint arrowheads; and he is more than glad to yield this area to Lankey so that he himself can claim another bank, church, or school; for, as Mathews sarcastically declares, "Christian Faith and Useful Knowledge came over as passengers, you know, with Captain Hudson" (24–25).

While Lankey's choice of property identifies him with a vanishing past, Big Abel's links him with an expansive, energetic present and future. This linkage is evidenced at the New York docks, where Big Abel appropriates to himself "the shipping to half a ton, with a boastful reference, I can tell you, to old Captain Hudson, who first of all the many ships lay in this port, you know" (68). Mathews describes the harbor through use of the classical catalogue technique, a device later used by Whitman, which captures the vibrancy of the scene:

And when they came out upon the water, there he stood, South Street!
Plenty of good warehouses, plenty of ships, plenty of pierheads! And seem-
ing to say all the time, "Here I am, South Street: and here I mean to be
for many a day to come. Don't be afraid to come along, ship, brig, schooner,
sloop, perogue, long-boat, cock-boat, jolly-boat: English, French, Dutch,
Russian, Norwegian, Kamschatkan—I'm ready. I've looked into the
matter a little, and know the state of this harbor pretty well. There's a
great variety of tonnage, I can tell you; and you may lay as deep as you
please without going to China. Come along!" And then he cocks his eye
toward the Narrows, on a sharp lookout for more sail: and how he rattles
his cordage and waves his streamers when a spanking wind comes in!
(67–68)

Tying Big Abel to such a scene throws him into sharp contrast with
Little Manhattan.

Though Lankey and Big Abel have opposing sets of values—one
dwelling predominantly in the past, the other in the present and
the future—it seems that the consummate epic vision of the
American experience would combine both outlooks, linking past
and future. Invariably, though, as we hurtle into the future, the past
is forgotten; for doing so is human nature and the Little Manhattan's tragedy. Mathews seems to be saying that, although it is
wrong to live in the past, as Lankey does, an American should be
aware of his national heritage. Perhaps Big Abel, though he does
care too much for the material wealth of the present, comes closest
to attaining this epic vision while, at the same time, he embodies it
in his own huge person; and he stands arms akimbo, like the
Whitman of *Leaves of Grass,* "a kosmos, of Manhattan the son,"
as he surveys his property: the towering steeples, the roads that
run the length of the island, and the bridges that he envisions as one
day reaching to Brooklyn and New Jersey. As he speaks of these
things his stature visibly increases.

Big Abel grows but Little Manhattan declines; and indeed he
cannot resist the hope that some downfall will be visited upon the
city and that it might again be "the old dear wilderness" of quiet
ledges and dark forest paths. Mathews speaks to the Indian:

The city grows; but you decline, I fear. . . . You still wander as a shade, the
city-hills, the city-slopes; sit sadly down by milestones as the city grows;
stand by the river's side, seeing there, what no other eye may see; dwindling
like a spirit to the city's eye, while he, Big Abel, waxes on sturdier by

every street he walks; by every square he builds. . . . Often [you withdraw] too, into that little village of Manhattanville at the Island's farthest point—it is said—for long, long spells. (92)

Little Manhattan, although largely neglected, will linger like the Mound-builders and Wakondah, as part of a national heritage which proud Americans can draw upon and find sustenance in—if only they stop casting their eyes and thoughts toward Europe.

V   *A Thanksgiving Story*

Although not aspiring to epic proportions, *Chanticleer; A Thanksgiving Story of the Peabody Family* (1850) also makes use of the American past in an effort to inspire readers with a sense of contemporary America's being just one phase in an organic, continuing epic. The Peabodys and their relations are average, middle-class "Every-Americans"; but in the noble bearing of their patriarchal grandfather, Sylvester, and in his patriotic tales of native history, we see that the average American is part of a continuum deriving from the Founding Fathers. Sylvester hopes to keep his family aware of this heritage and tries to give them a code, based on heroic examples from the national past, to live by.

In his preface, Mathews emphasizes the nationalistic aims of his "little holiday book," which "is in harmony with that cherished answering," Thanksgiving. He hopes that his work may be received as a "kindly word spoken to all classes and sections of his [Mathews'] fellow citizens, awakening a feeling of union and fraternal friendship at this genial season."[11] Endeavoring to carry out these aims, Mathews depicts the Peabody home as the prototype of American homes throughout the nation, characterizing it as the "Old Homestead" which "lies on the map in the heart of one of the early states of our dear American union" (10).

As typical Americans, the Peabodys have a part in the proud national heritage. Sylvester speaks of the memories that the Thanksgiving holiday and the Indian summer weather conjure up. He recalls the absent and the dead, those who fell by his side in battle or while working in their fields; and he thanks God that all of his people died "with names untouched with crime." In speaking of the past, he provides anecdotes of the heroism shown by the simple, homely men who fought in the American Revolution, men such as Ethan Barbary, a preacher who also did his part as a soldier, who never forgot the lessons of charity he had learned and taught as a man of God, and who selflessly devoted his life to tending the sick and needy. As a soldier, he showed courage that belied his mildness in peacetime; and he fought bravely while sharing his gun with another soldier, for they had only one between them.

Such tales of experiences shared by Sylvester aggrandize him and the average American he epitomizes, but the patriarch realizes that his life is nearly over and leaves his family an injunction from the past. Calling himself "one of the few stalks that still remain in the field where the tempest passed," he declares that he fought against the foreigners for the sake of his descendants and that he won freedom for them. Consequently, he urges them not to disappoint him in his old age by "abandoning the path" he would have them follow, one of moral rectitude which he believes will lead to a prosperous, happy America that will attain the glories of its manifest destiny. He sees his happy family, made up of relatives from all over America, as emblematic of "our glorious family of friendly states, [which] on this and every other day, [can] join hands, and like happy children in the fields, lead a far-lengthening dance of festive peace . . . from the soft-glimmering east far on to the bright and ruddy west" (99–100). Not an epic, itself, *Chanticleer* is a celebration of the largest epic—the United States.

VI   *The American Witch Hunt*

Mathews' *Witchcraft*, produced in New York in 1847, is a poetic drama dealing with the Salem witch hunts which provides a sound basis for Sylvester Peabody's claim that the American land has been paid for by the blood and suffering of many decent people. The courage and dignity of those who confronted the hysteria and were executed for their heroism present an example for all Americans to follow.

The dramatic interest in *Witchcraft* derives from the contrast between characters like Deacon Gidney, Officer Pudeater, and Jarvis Dane, who foster the hysteria; like Susanna Peache, who allows herself to be driven by it; and those like Gideon Bodish and his mother, Ambla, who oppose it and are victimized by it. Mathews effects a powerful tension between the forces of repression and the desire for individual freedom, thus attempting to bring his contemporaries to an awareness of the efforts of their forebears on behalf of the cause of human rights. Working to this end, he creates several strongly delineated characters and imbues their actions with the requisite sense of national significance.

Heading the forces of hate and superstition in Salem are Deacon Gidney, one of the spiritual leaders of the community, and Officer Pudeater, Salem's police chief. In Gidney, Mathews captures the essential quality of the fanatic whose misguided fervor sets an atmosphere of bigotry and fear which inevitably leads to the tormenting of innocent people. We first learn of Gidney through an old friend's reminiscences of him as a boy:

> Yes of good heart for work that's toward—
> Be sure that he, who when a stripling boy,
> Did strike a wicked woman of four score,
> For kneeling not when his good father called
> To prayer, will not delay to sharply deal
> With sorcery now.[12]

On the other hand, Gidney's henchman Pudeater has no principles save those of self-preservation and self-advancement. Consequently, the man who should provide at least a semblance of civil authority in Salem's theocracy merely serves as an eager informer who willingly spies on and harasses old women in order that he might secure a raise in pay, declaring that he'll "pry through key-holes to overhear their talk," for if he can catch even one witch, he will "be made forever" (12). In this town, then, which has lost its sense of decency, all that is needed for systematic persecution to begin is for one individual to declare his suspicion of another. The accuser in *Witchcraft* is Jarvis Dane, who plots against the Bodishes because Susanna, the girl he loves, is infatuated with Gideon.

Fortunately for Jarvis' purposes, Gideon and Ambla Bodish are extremely vulnerable to accusation, for their strange, solitary way of life can easily lead a whole community of conformists to turn against them. The Bodishes, who reside quietly on the edge of the forest, discourage any offers of friendship. Furthermore, their isolation results in great part from Ambla's increasingly frequent practice of walking the dark forests alone and of muttering softly to herself all the while. Ambla is also known to make little clay figures representing Salem's leaders, which, it is thought, she uses for conjuring. Though Gideon is appalled by his mother's behavior, he changes the pattern of his own life so that he can give her the help and protection he believes that she needs. Consequently, Gideon, too, becomes a recluse whose life causes comment among other Salemites. Gideon's old friend, Topsfield, remarks of him and his mother:

> I would go many miles and often,
> To make him cheerfuller: I fear, I know,
> There's something sad and strange beneath that roof—
> Depend upon't—it makes me sad to think so.
> He has not loved, no maiden can avow it;
> He has not wived, no children sit upon his knee;
> His whole soul's tide has set one way, and washes
> Forever that large shore, a mother's love. (14–15)

Taking advantage of Ambla and Gideon's bad reputation in the village, Jarvis Dane spreads vile rumors about them; and their neighbors soon report seeing them ride the clouds, whose pace and direction, they claim, Ambla can control. When a delegation, headed by Deacon Gidney, goes to the Bodishes' home to inquire into their strange practices and confronts Ambla, who is alone, Gidney demands to know why she has not been attending church. Her response is a defense of the individual's right to choose his own form of worship: "there is a silent service, sir, I've heard/It said, keeps up its worship at the heart,/Although the lips be closed." Gideon, appearing at this moment, vehemently defends his mother against Gidney's charges of witchcraft; indeed, he accuses Gidney and his kind of being the actual perpetrators of evil. His attack on Gidney is couched in terms of a defense of freedom in a new, unspoiled land, thus showing again that one of Mathews' chief concerns in this play is an effort to instill into his audience a sense of America as a place of special promise:

> 'Tis you who do the devil's work most eagerly,
> Why defile you this fresh new world, this air
> That blossoms sweetly, unmoved by any
> But the blest presence of free men and things
> As free—with droppings of your filthy hands? (35)

The importance of this idea for Mathews is apparent when Gideon's speech is echoed by the comments of an old immigrant who, to flee tyranny, had recently arrived in the New World. He speaks of the blight being placed on the land as a result of the witch hunt. To the immigrant, the American landscape is sacred; and, like Mathews, he believes this fact must be impressed upon his countrymen. Bearing Mathews' explicit message for America, the immigrant foresees a glorious future "when this young land goes free" and will become a nation of liberty, unlike any other. However, he warns Salem's bigots, "you and such as you, will soil its beauty to the latest ages" (44); and Mathews is making clear to his audience that the good times they now enjoy are not the result of happenstance but the products of hard fights against injustice. Moreover, the implication running through *Witchcraft,* as it does through all of Mathews' works which deal with the American past, is that the memory of such fights must be kept alive if the nation is to retain a sense of its identity.

Ambla's defense of individual choice of worship and Gideon's attack on Gidney only add to the townspeoples' impression of their guilt, and charges are soon brought against Ambla. The Bodishes find they are alone in their efforts to defend themselves: Gideon's old friends turn against him and his mother, and even Susanna is prevailed upon by Jarvis to testify against Ambla. Jarvis has convinced her that, if she helps convict Ambla, Gideon might be removed from his mother's evil influence and return Susanna's love. However, as Jarvis shrewdly assesses the situation, he realizes that, when Ambla is found guilty, as assuredly she will be, it will be only a short time until Gideon is also.

As the trial draws near, we learn that Gideon has for some time suspected his mother of evil deeds—perhaps even of witchcraft. Indeed, he has almost convicted her in his own mind; however, he has stood by her all the while and, presumably, would continue to do so despite his suspicions. Shortly before the trial, though, seemingly supernatural events occurring in the Bodish home lead Gideon to declare his suspicions to his mother. He senses an apparition in the house, and suddenly his mother's Bible flies open to the words, "set thine house in order, for thou shalt die." Ambla says it is a "better spirit" sent by God, but Gideon sees the words, "A Witch" flaming in the air. He accuses his mother of wrongdoing, and this leads her to explain her strange behavior of the past. She confesses that Gideon's father was killed in a duel with a man he had suspected of being her illicit lover. The man was not her lover, and Ambla could have proved it; but, since her pride was hurt, she had let her husband take part in the duel to see him punished for his suspicions. Since his death, she has been tormented by guilt; a reaction which accounts for her strange ways. Gideon, touched by his mother's confession, has a renewed faith in her innocence.

Seemingly, the apparition, which Mathews never explains, was either conjured up by Gideon's suspicions or was a beneficent spirit sent to precipitate the accusations that would lead to a reconciliation between mother and son. In fact, Ambla believes that in America, a new, as yet unsullied land, beneficent spirits are close to man:

> Spirits possess the earth 'till men, cities
> And habitations of gross clay uprear thereon:
> They haunt this uncontaminated scene
> More than old regions with their towers,
> And smoky streets, and angry piles of war,
> From the old time these things have been, and shall
> They be no more? Spirits affect, or may,
> This beautiful fair land, dewy and new,
> And suitable, in dark or bright, to their blest ways. (82)

The trial, transpiring as it does shortly after the Bodishes' reconciliation, seems all the more vile, for we see it even more clearly as simply additional torment for an already troubled old woman. However, Mathews uses the trial not merely as an attack on fear and bigotry but also as a means of establishing Gideon as a representative American hero—as a man of dignity and courage. Thus, Gideon, refusing to beg for mercy, attempts to recall his townsmen to a sense of manly honor:

> I ask you, here and now—will you permit
> This judgement to o'erwhelm an ancient head—
> The whitest, noblest, the most reverend head
> Of Salem? Ye cannot be so lost, so drifted
> Far away from what you were and should be;
> Call back that doom—repeal the bigot's voice,
> And stand up here, full-statured, men of Salem! (91)

Gideon realizes, as his speech has no effect and as his mother is convicted, that these men are beyond talk of honor. Consequently, he knows that he must act alone, and he shouts that he will not allow his mother to suffer the ignominy of being hanged:

> Aye, cut me down and her; tear us in pieces—
> Trample beneath your feet with demon power,
> And rack us as you will, in baffled hate—
> She shall not die the felon's tainted death!
> . . . .
> See you,—a mother, here, most pure, most holy,
> And here, a son, whose heart leaves its red bank,
> Against your coming—advance upon us!
> Here's merely age and youth, against you all—
> A verdict of our own we make, a death
> To die, above your blind and bigot law! (97)

While attempting to defend his mother, Gideon is stabbed to death by Jarvis; and Ambla dies of shock. At the same time, word arrives that Susanna has killed herself; thus has Jarvis' plan had larger effects than even he could have predicted.

In *Witchcraft,* Mathews, in addition to attacking bigotry, is also praising America: first, by emphasizing that there is something pure and beautiful in the land, making it closer to God than is the Old World; second, by presenting Ambla and Gideon as strong-willed individuals who refuse to truckle before a corrupt authority. Their qualities of pride, loyalty, and honor are what Mathews emphasizes as the best parts of the American heritage which permeates the atmosphere of American life.

In its use of native history in an effort to show Americans that their national heritage is a proud one, *Witchcraft* carries out aims similar to those in *Behemoth, Wakondah, Big Abel and the Little Manhattan,* and *Chanticleer.* Running through all of these works is Mathews' theme that Americans ought to be aware of their heroic predecessors and of the grandeur of the present (made even grander by the influence of the past); for such awareness will inevitably predicate a glorious destiny for the country. This theme is conveyed, generally, through creating an "epic" from the materials of American history, as in *Behemoth* and *Wakondah;* through describing the epical interaction of past and present, as in *Big Abel and the Little Manhattan;* or, finally, through simply providing examples of past heroism, as in *Chanticleer* and *Witchcraft,* which aggrandize the American experience—an actual epic in its own right.

VII *A "Rude Vigor of Thought"*

Mathews' effort on behalf of his countrymen, although an admirable one, is relatively unsuccessful from a literary standpoint; for these works are frequently clumsy, maudlin, and slovenly written. However, it would be shortsighted to view him simply as a literary eccentric whose conceptions so far exceed his grasp as to render him ludicrous. He is a product of his era, and in his work we can see mid-nineteenth-century America groping toward an expression of its national experience. In 1835, de Tocqueville, the perceptive French observer of America, described the frame of mind of which Mathews is a manifestation; claiming that, although Americans have no poets, they are not without poetic ideas. The American people, he contends, are constantly aware of their "own march across [the continental] wilds,—drying swamps, turning the course of rivers, peopling solitudes, and subduing nature."[13] In every action that he takes, each American is haunted by this heroic image of himself as the world's pioneer who conducts a heroic struggle against the forces of nature. Whether this state of mind was typical of most Americans at the time is problematical; but Mathews, who had it, tried desperately to share his vision with his countrymen.

Furthermore, de Tocqueville, when he speaks of the largeness of the democratic poet's vision in America, asserts that, because all the citizens in a democratic society are nearly equal and alike, it is difficult for the poet to dwell upon any one of them; therefore, he writes of the nation itself. Making this a more practicable undertaking is the clear perception that democratic nations have of their own aspect. They are able to generalize about themselves more accurately than other nations are (181). Such large perceptions make for imposing literary subjects, which explains why the scope of Mathews' vision is so large.

Finally, de Tocqueville believes that literary style in America is, and generally will continue to be, rough and uncouth. A democratic society does not lend itself as readily as does an aristocracy to artistic principles of order, regularity, and science. Instead, its authors write in a manner which is frequently "fantastic, incorrect, overburdened, and loose" but "almost always vehement and bold." He foresees an American literature which will, by very nature of its being democratic, "bear marks of an untutored and rude vigor of thought" (177). These remarks by de Tocqueville are applicable to much of Mathews' work because he tried to write for the democracy he loved. Mathews' literary failures, therefore, although flagrant, must be seen against the backdrop of the national context of which he was a part in order to be put into their proper perspective. The literary shortcomings of Mathews' historical works are, to be sure, often glaring; but the magnitude of his effort makes these works significant despite their faults.

CHAPTER 4

The Development of a "Sense of Place"

I *The Local Ambiance*

THE use of native historical materials to create an epic description of American life and to call attention to the actual epic that America is itself is only part of Mathews' effort to persuade his countrymen to look at their nation and to write about it with freshness and originality. In addition to working with national history, he turns to a depiction of real life in his contemporary America and provides enough descriptive material to force upon his readers a sense of lived American life. His many descriptive passages are like blocks of environmental material to be assimilated by the reader, not primarily because of any significance they may have in relation to the plot, but because of their importance in conveying the atmosphere or ambiance of specific aspects of the American scene.

Through passages describing his contemporary America, Mathews carries out what William Carlos Williams called in *Paterson* a "celebration of the place." Mathews, like Williams, moves from a mass of particulars to a general picture extolling the environment or, using Williams' phrase, "celebrating it." Indeed, we see in Mathews' efforts to create what, for want of a better term, I shall call a "sense of place," a rudimentary form of Williams' objectivism. Williams describes his method in *Paterson:*

> To make a start,
> out of particulars
> and make them general, rolling
> up the sum, by defective means—[1]

He calls this process one of achieving "by multiplication a reduction to one." Later he asserts, "Say it, no ideas but in things—/nothing but the blank faces of houses/and cylindrical trees" (11). This method is not unlike Mathews' method of portraying America—that of providing local description merely for the sake of description, with little plot relevance, in order to convey an almost tangible sense of the locality he is exploring and to depict some of the scenes out of which an overall picture of America can be created. Such scenes are in evidence in all of Mathews' works, but they seem to be most prominent, almost to the extent of serving as each work's *raison d'être,* in *The Motley Book, Big Abel and the Little Manhattan,* and *A Pen-and-Ink Panorama of New York City.*

In Mathews' repeated emphasis on capturing the peculiar flavors of specific American locales, he follows in the Knicker-bocker tradition established by Irving and Paulding; but he adds to it, as well, by describing more of the unpleasant and often sordid aspects of the local scene than his New York predecessors (or a New York contemporary, Nathaniel Parker Willis, who de-picted local scenes) ever did. Moreover, unlike Hawthorne, whose description of Massachusetts scenes was often a vehicle for deeper, spiritual concerns, Mathews describes native scenes with the sole purpose of showing his readers their country and compatriots. Consequently, along with such a delineator of western scenes as Caroline Kirkland, Mathews comes closer than most of his contem-poraries to presaging the local colorists of the next generation; and, although Mathews' form of "local color," which is both of the city and the country, is occasionally not quite as realistic as that of the regional sketches to come, he does, however, match them frequently in delineating the quality of everyday life in a specific area as well as in capturing the picturesque and strange there. Indeed, some of Mathews' scenes of city life at its grimmest seem to point ahead to such late nineteenth-century depictions of sordid urban milieus in Stephen Crane's *Maggie* and Frank Norris' *McTeague.*

Interestingly enough, Mathews' effort to describe local scenes may have been influenced somewhat by the work of Charles Dickens. To the casual observer, it might seem that Mathews was thus rather hypocritical in vociferously demanding a distinctly Ameri-can literature, while being influenced at the same time by an English writer. However, Mathews was not a slavish imitator; rather, he was simply attempting to describe American scenes with the same veracity and color with which Dickens treated En-glish ones. Thus, in literature as in politics, nationalists and re-volutionaries may frequently use as their examples leaders and ideas of other nations.

II   The Motley Book

In *The Motley Book* (1838), a collection of tales and sketches by Mathews, we find numerous examples of Mathews' desire to create a "sense of place." The prefatory "To the Merry Reader" finds Mathews in the guise of "editor" telling of "the late Ben Smith," the supposed author of *The Motley Book*. Smith is characterized as a "merry author" full of "sparkling humor" and possessed of a "swift and keen vision for the ludicrous, and an ear open as day to a melting tale." The "neighbouring villages and counties . . . were *his* books and library, and out of them he read many pleasant passages which adorn these writings."[2] Mathews, in this collection, aims at showing his American readers what their world is and at making them aware that the "neighbouring villages and counties" are colorful and exciting; for, as a literary nationalist, he knows that surrounding reality must not be ignored.

The observations of the "late Ben Smith" are presented in *The Motley Book* as stories and sketches of both rural and urban scenes. Such items as "Beelzebub and His Cart," "Greasy Peterson," "The Melancholy Vagabond," and "The Great Charter Contest in Gotham" are exhibitions of city life in its various aspects; they capture many moods of the metropolis and depict different levels of its society. Rural scenes provide the settings for "The Adventures of Sol Clarion," "The Merry Makers," and "The Disasters of Old Drudge," which, like the city pieces, are attempts to convey the flavor of a region and its way of life.

"Beelzebub and His Cart" relates the story of a huge New York City Negro who drives a garbage wagon which serves as a front for his more nefarious activities as a receiver of stolen goods. After a while, the people along Beelzebub's route realize where their lost goods have been going; and they chase this "Imp of Darkness," as they call him, until he eludes them and arrives safely in Westchester County, a suburb of New York City. Here, he meets a little old man who claims to be the ghost of the last Dutch schoolmaster of New York. The old man drowns Beelzebub, steals his wagon and loot, and rides away to Long Island where he and the cart "can still be heard trampling down the great Jamaica Turnpike."[3]

As is apparent from the brief synopsis of "Beelzebub," there is little of merit in the story line. What *is* of some merit, though, is Mathews' depiction of local scenes. Through his description of the neighborhood in which Beelzebub works and its inhabitants, we learn something of the way of life in that district. We see a dim-witted "keystone cop" of a policeman, and two large, loud women who complain vociferously and bully their husbands in an atmosphere pervaded with stupidity and greed. This scene is juxtaposed against the Westchester landscape into which Beelzebub escapes, a scene of pastoral calm and beauty, given an added aura of the strange and picturesque by the presence of the legendary Dutch schoolmaster. Thus, through his juxtaposition of these two New York scenes, Mathews, without ever explicitly stating one, effects a moral judgment in which he seems to condemn the crassness and vulgarity which taint part of New York life.

In "Greasy Peterson," a short, retrospective sketch of a "smooth, unctuous, fish-faced" grocer, Mathews does little more than describe a local type, the shrewd merchant-trader, and the implications are that he was the sort of person who ought not to go unnoticed either in actual life or in any literature purporting to have relevance to real life. Peterson's most memorable character trait was the quickness of his business sense, which made him something of a neighborhood legend. Like the shifty horse traders observed in humorous scenes of the Old Southwest, "Greasy Bob" Peterson had numerous dodges in order to get the best of a trade. Frequently, he went to the wharves in "rude garments and vagabond presentment" in order to dupe unwary boatmen and merchants. Knowing that they would think him a mere tramp, he invariably asked the price of some commodity. The bargain might then be struck to his advantage if the dealer believed in appearances as readily as one captain did:

"Why loafer," replied the captain of the sloop, to whom this question was addressed in a slouching, careless tone, "why uncle oily-breeches, I guess *you* may have it six pence a pound the lot."

"I'll take it sir!" said Greasy Peterson, throwing an air of considerable seriousness and dignity into his remark, which startled the rash butter-merchant slightly.

"But mind ye neighbor—it's cash down at that price! Come fork over the solid, Old Rags," said the boatman, with a loud laugh, and turning with a quizzical leer to a group of captains and sloopboys that had gathered to see the fun.[4]

Naturally, Greasy, who had cash on hand, turned a tidy profit and enjoyed the final laugh. When, after years of artful maneuvering, Peterson died of apoplexy, the neighborhood lost a wonderful conversation piece. It is such native conversation pieces that Mathews believes an American writer cannot afford to ignore without vitiating his work and turning his back on his country.

A less amusing local type, the New York City political hack, is delineated in "The Melancholy Vagabond." Neddy Budge, the "vagabond" of the title, is a quondam machine politician fallen on bad times. Mathews describes Neddy's public career: "He had opened life as a constable in a fifty dollar court. From his humble position on the floor of the court-room, clearing the bar and bawling 'to order!' he had, one lucky day, by a sudden change of parties and favour with political leaders, found his way to the Justice's seat, and there he presided for many years a legal dark-lantern, by whose uncertain and wavering light many an unfortunate plaintiff or defendant was plunged into a pit of costs" (60). Fortune then turned again, and he was reduced once more to a constable; after another turn, he became the court janitor; and, finally, he lost even that job, ending up a disconsolate vagabond fisherman. The attempts of friends to cheer him by talking of past triumphs—such as the case in which he "threatened one of the defendant's witnesses [that] if he didn't stop snivelling in court [Neddy, the judge] would send him up to the Dry Dock to be new caulked"—prove ineffectual; and the melancholy vagabond, no longer having an eminent position in this world, leaves it by hanging himself (62).

The brief glimpse of the New York political scene which Mathews gives us in "The Melancholy Vagabond" is amplified in "The Great Charter Contest in Gotham," a sketch which captures the boisterous energy as well as the frequent ludicrousness of a big-city election. Mathews delights in observing that "particular season of the year in the city of New York‹ when ragamuffins and vagabonds take a sudden rise in respectability" (79), when a spurious air of democratic camaraderie ranks a "tarpaulin hat" as high as the "crown of an emperor," and when "the uncombed locks of a wharf rat or river vagrant [are] looked upon with as much veneration as if they belonged to Apollo in his brightest moments of inspiration" (79).

The contest which prompts this show of brotherhood is between two perennial types of American political office-seekers: the patrician defender of stability and the rabble-rousing plebeian. Herbert

Hickock, "Esquire," dressed in an immaculate, gentlemanly manner, sallies forth from his fashionable residence every morning; but his opponent, Bill Snivel, a retired shoemaker, delights in projecting an image of uncouthness. The great principles on which their warfare is waged are, "on the one hand, that tidy apparel is an indisputable evidence of a foul and corrupt code of principles; and on the other, that to be poor and unclean denotes a total deprivation of the reasoning faculties." The course of action, therefore, for each party becomes clear. The Snivel party must "discover Mr. Hickock in some act of personal uncleanliness or cacography," while the Hickock supporters endeavor to detect Snivel "in the use of good English or unexceptionable linen" (80).

Mathews, in keeping with his aim of carefully describing local customs and mores, points up the distinctive qualities of each party's meetings, even finding distinguishing features as to the type of noise each group makes: "With regard to the noises which now and then emanated from the lungs of the respective assemblages—there was more music in the shouts and vociferations of the Hickock meetings—more vigour and rough energy in the Bill Snivel. If a zoological distinction might be made, the Bill Snivel voice resembled that of a cage-full of hungry young tigers slightly infuriated, while the Hickock seemed to be modelled on the clamour of an old lion after dinner" (81).

Next, we get a look at the chicanery involved in "getting out the vote" during the three days of actual balloting. At one polling place an inebriated hobo, who presents himself as a Snivel voter to be sworn in by the inspector, is challenged by a Hickock poll watcher, who shouts, "Ask him if he understands the nature of an oath." "What is an oath?" asks the inspector. The Snivel voter's response, "Damn your eyes!" indicates that he knows its nature (84). Such vignettes as that at the polling place, and one in which two rival canvassers fight over a still-prone drunkard just fished from the East River, evoke for the reader the humor and frenzy of a New York election, providing him with an awareness of one part of the American experience with which he may be unfamiliar, or which he may have taken for granted. Such "local color," Mathews believes, American readers and authors should not take for granted; it is part of their world and helps determine their lives.

In "The Adventures of Sol Clarion" Mathews turns *The Mot-*

ley Book from its depiction of urban life and looks to rural scenes. Sol and his half-witted friend, Will Robin, are bumpkins who become involved in a lawsuit to win control of a farm from Sol's uncle. Their story is worth noting only insofar as it serves Mathews as a vehicle for establishing a "sense of place," evoking for his readers the tenor of rural life, which he accomplishes both through description of natural scenery and exhibition of local characters. As Will and Sol, out for a Sunday ride, relax near a pond, Mathews describes the idyllic scene: "Before Sol as he sat upon a jutting rock, embowered in trees, the cheek of the sweet pond swelled with the curve and fullness of beauty itself; kissed by forest shadows that here and there fall like caresses from the wavering trees. Now and then a stray duck started out from the shore, and flew, like a silent thought, back into its native element. Afar the meadows stretched and swelled into gentle hills, which lay basking in the sun, with an ox or horse now and then stealing quietly across the landscape" (32).

Unfortunately, Sol and Will make the mistake of straying from such charming landscapes to the murky bogs of Sol's lawsuit. This blunder is compounded by Sol's choice of a lawyer, the ancient Peter Doublet, one of those men occasionally found in small towns who is grotesquely out of touch with the times. The "best part of his life had lain in the eighteenth century . . . , all his thoughts and feelings dated back forty years. He saw every object through time's telescope inverted." Mathews, attempting to give a full, concrete description of this type of man, provides a detailed picture of Doublet's clothing, the style of which gives insight into the nature of its owner. A "well-preserved model of mortality," he wears a flowing white wig "like that in the portrait of Sir Isaac Newton"; a black velvet coat with silver buttons; shirts stiffened with buckram; a scarlet vest; and "a set of white small clothes joining black silk hose, and huge silver buttons." Mathews declares that Doublet "still preserved and strictly maintained the vesture and habits of the last century, and obstinately refused to lay aside the smallest tittle or thread of his dress, or to abate a single jot of the severity of ancient manners" (34).

This living antique's knowledge of the law is as outmoded as his physical appearance. He declares that he will take possession of the contested farm "by livery of seisin under the old law, (the d——l taking if he please, lease and release, and such modern traps and tricks of pettifoggers)" (36). By the "old law" he means the one before the American Revolution; however, as Doublet and the plaintiff find when they arrive at the farm in question, the old law is no longer particularly efficacious, for the outraged uncle drives them off after hearing of the livery of seisin, by plying a cudgel and shouting, "I'll give your liver a seasoning—you lout!" (41).

The failure of their plans prompts Sol and Will to leave the country to try their luck in New York City. On their stagecoach trip, they meet a peculiarly American type, a cross between P. T. Barnum and a raucous backwoodsman of the Old Southwest. He boards the coach carrying a gamecock and introduces himself as Paul Hyaena Patchell, "Keeper of a wild beast show, and the greatest collection of natural wonders now extant in the four quarters!" Mathews transcribes his speech:

"I have been scouring the country for a five legged calf to complete my collection, or a cow with the horns growing upon her flanks! Confound the stupid creatures, they put me out. I couldn't as much as even find one with a moderate swelling to pass for a dromedary. Nevertheless I've met with a little success . . . gentlemen, I have picked up a game cock with a face just like General Jackson. See! . . . every line's distinct—here's the warlike nose, the warrior eye and" at this moment one of the legs of the interesting creature slipped from his hand and dashed two thirds of a spur into the smart showman's wrist, who exclaimed, smiling faintly, "by the Bengal lion the general has just drawn his sword!" (45)

Unhappily, after this promising beginning, the adventures of Sol and Will and the account of the people they meet are not continued; and, except for one unimportant vignette, Mathews fails to explore the potential of the traditional situation in which a country rube goes to the big city. However, "The Adventures of Sol Clarion" is moderately successful in portraying several aspects of rural life, such as the beautiful peace of a summer afternoon in the woods, and the pictures of the eccentric antiquarian, the bluff, no-nonsense farmer, and the traveling showman.

Another fixture of the rural landscape is presented in "The Merry-Makers. Exploit No. I," which describes the pranks of a group of fun-loving hellions who roam around the countryside exulting in making themselves objectionable to "respectable folks" in a manner more fully developed later by G. W. Harris' Sut Lovingood.

Mathews, serving in his role as delineator of local types and customs, declares that they are "roaring boys . . . [with] something of the swaggerer in their composition, whose exploits are part of the history, and their mirthful speeches part of the vernacular of country villages and neighborhoods" (65). We find the Merry-Makers at a meeting in "a dilapidated and ancient outhouse," where they are planning their next exploit. Their leader, Bobbylink, declares, "I think we had better forego the project of tapping Uncle Aaron's cider barrels today. The liquor will be better a month or two hence. I have a better game to propose" (65). It is a game to get them a feast, for they have all been complaining of empty bellies, as Sam Chisel, one of Bobbylink's lieutenants, declares:

Your sarvant . . . has attended three houses raisin's: two weddin's and one christenin', come off with a dry belly from all six. For why? One man fell down dead wid an opoplexy, the furst mug of cider he swallered; 'cordingly the barrels was all spiked for fear of fudder accidents; the other two raisin's was on the rock crystal, cold water plan; the baby at the christenin' was two small herself for to eat, 'cordingly they giv' nothin' out; the two weddin's was over when I got there—'cause why? Bak Viol told me the wrong hour. (66)

Such a speech reveals that Mathews must have read the Jack Downing letters as well as the other native humorists of the time, for its use of vernacular parallels their methods and anticipates those of the local colorists. Furthermore, in addition to providing a colorful example of the vernacular, Sam's account describes some of the rural customs which Mathews wants to exhibit for his readers.

Bobbylink and his "wild fellows" plan to assuage their hunger by taking advantage of the local superstition that a deceased Jewish clothes peddler haunts the region; and Bobbylink and his crew disguise themselves in the more outlandish costumes left in his deserted house. In this garb, they descend upon the guests at a wedding feast, frightening them off, and gorge themselves on the hurriedly deserted food. Mathews is careful to include realistic details in the scene, to keep the readers remembering that he is describing a specific American locale. Consequently, we are told that the marauders must make do without eating utensils because "according to an ancient custom that prevails in that region, the wedding company had established themselves at the table before the knives and forks were laid at the plates: that being a service generally rendered by a negro or maid-servant immediately after grace"

(76). Because of the timing of their attack, the maidservant ran off before placing the silverware. Such a detail is not of tremendous importance, but it does point out that Mathews is attempting to observe the American scene closely and perhaps, through doing so, serve as an example for other American authors.

Bobbylink and his friends are seen again in "The Merry-Makers. Exploit No. II," in which Bobby courts a lovely dairymaid, Hetty Settle. In the vicissitudes of their courtship we see many of the elements which have come to be associated with nineteenth-century native American humor, such as the scheming of the suitor to get his girl to consent to his proposal and the practical jokes of the friends who disrupt the proceedings.

Mathews begins this tale with a long description of the bucolic scene in which Bob and Hetty are carrying out their deliberations of love. His nature description here combines an accurate representation of some grim details (the dead water-fly and caught fish) with studiously romantic idealization in an attempt to portray both the actual environment and the penchant of lovers to see their own feelings reflected in their surroundings:

Near by on some neighboring rail, two amorous catbirds chatter away in animated discourse, hopping along the fence in flight and pursuit—a precious pair of ill-dressed, vagrant lovers: while, far off on the edge of the lake, so their puny heads are just visible, bobbing up and down, two friendly little snipes are paying their respects to each other over a dead water-fly. In a thorn-bush a sweet-tempered brown thrasher hurries through his joyous and flute-like song, as if he were afraid the day would be over ere he could disburthen half his music. The love-lorn king-fisher hangs on a dry bough over the stream, and brawls in his harsh, startling voice, determined to outroar the current, and keeping an eye fixed on the surface: the moment an unhappy fish becomes visible this aquatic bailiff springs upon him, fastens a talon on his shoulder, and flying to a retired quarter consoles himself for the absence of his mistress. (141)

Reclining in the midst of this scene, Bob, urging Hetty to marry him, uses as his chief enticement the hoax that his rich, old grandmother is dying and that he will be fondly remembered in her will. Hetty guesses, however, that there is no such grandmother; but she declares that she will marry Bob anyway on condition that he forsake his old friends, whom she sees as a disreputable bunch who get him into trouble. Bob readily agrees with her; he even outdoes

Hetty in enumerating their faults and claims that he will not even invite them to the wedding.

Unfortunately, the courtship agreement is overheard by the rest of the Merry-Makers, who, determining to have revenge, receive an immediate opportunity as Bob and Hetty row about the neighboring lake. Playing on a local story about a "laughing devil" who haunts the surrounding woods, they set up an eerie, shrieking laughter while deftly pushing Bob and Hetty off, without oars, toward a waterfall. Then they get out on the lake, themselves, and give the unlucky pair a dunking. Fortunately, the lovers realize that they have been foolishly haughty, and all have a good laugh over the situation.

In both the "Merry-Maker" stories, we see Mathews trying to capture the comedy and boisterous energy of rural life in a manner somewhat similar to that of only a few of his contemporaries, such as Seba Smith and Judge Longstreet. In the satirical piece "The Disasters of Old Drudge," however, Mathews paints a less pleasant picture of rural life. The story of hen-pecked Old Drudge and of his comic misadventures serves as the vehicle for Mathews' description of the town of Plumpitts, an ugly place full of small people who indulge in crass bickering and gossip; Mathews speaks of "pestilent old women" who spend their time in "wholesaling scandal and small talk to each other—and a very thriving trade they make of it" (152). He then describes the rest of the village's inhabitants: "The standing population . . . is composed of about twenty bluenosed topers who hover about a place called the Point, like so many noisy gulls, during the early part of the morning and towards night, and pass the rest of the day in dirty fishing boats along the shore of the Sound, solemnly engaged in capturing blackfish and bass for their present wants, and providing a stock of cramps and rheumatisms for their old age" (152).

Epitomizing the sordidness and ugliness of this blighted area is the farm of Old Drudge and his shrewish wife. They live in a "dilapidated old house," styled "the Homestead," which is set on an "ill-conditioned piece of land" (152). In the house we encounter Drudge "bent nearly double over a bowl of sour buttermilk, and a white earthen plate, holding a single, small perch or sunfish, burned to a crisp" (153). This picture of the unpleasant aspects of rural life is not unlike that given by Whittier in his preface to "Among the Hills."

Sent into town on an errand by his wife (she has locked him in his coach so that he will not stop at the tavern), Old Drudge is set upon by his many town-based creditors and by his villainous boy servant in a riotous scene which soon turns into a violent free-for-all by the townspeople and a mad dash home for Drudge as his unattended horse bolts and carries the coach on a careening course around the countryside. The old man arrives home; and, "bruised, frightened and hungry as he is, he is glad to hobble upstairs and sneak supperless to bed, rather than encounter one of those domestic 'tempests' which rattle about him so often" (167).

"The Disasters of Old Drudge" counterbalances the idealized picture of rural life which Mathews presents in other sketches in *The Motley Book.* By using Old Drudge as his focal point and by showing the response to his timidity of those around him, Mathews depicts the harsh, ugly aspects of country life as it often is in reality. Thus, in *The Motley Book,* Mathews presents scenes of both urban and rural life in an endeavor to bring his readers' attention to their environment and to show his fellow writers that the American landscape is replete with subject matter for writers who will take the time actually to look at it, as did "the late Ben Smith."

III *"A Mid-Century Panorama"*

Seven years later, in his attempted epic *Big Abel and the Little Manhattan,* Mathews again endeavors to evoke for his readers the American scene, the New York City area in particular, with little reference to the surrounding countryside. Because of this work's epic pretensions, it is even more important for Mathews to provide a sense of place; for an epic must convey an aura of the total environment of which the characters are a representation and in which they act. Consequently, in *Big Abel and the Little Manhattan,* even more than in *The Motley Book,* we note environmental description which exists simply for the sake of providing a vivid depiction of the locale. Also, there is more local description in this work than in Mathews' other epic, *Behemoth,* because *Big Abel*'s New York City setting offers more possibilities for sketches of the picturesque than does the relatively barren landscape of the Mound-builders' country (which Mathews carefully described, anyway, in keeping with his epic designs). Moreover, *Big Abel*'s setting is a contemporary one which Mathews believes has been taken for granted by most of his fellow city dwellers. Therefore, he wants to impress upon them that these scenes through which they pass each day are colorful and interesting; he wants to overwhelm them with the reality of the world in which they live and then ignore by turning to a foreign literature or to an effete, imitative native one. As another facet of this effort, Mathews, like the local colorists, also wants to show that environment, to a great extent, determines character; therefore, if one would know oneself and one's fellows, one must know the local environment.

The eerie opening scene of *Big Abel and the Little Manhattan,* which is set at the great, white Shot-Tower (described in the preceding chapter), creates an atmosphere in which the local is imbued with an air of strangeness and romance; and Mathews fosters this atmosphere throughout the book. For example, juxtaposed against the Shot-Tower scene is one in the Jewish district of lower Manhattan, an area which the average New Yorker might casually dismiss as too prosaic, if not too sordid, for literary interest. Yet, the romance of the Shot-Tower scene carries over into this one, permeating the Jewish district and making it suddenly picturesque:

He [Lankey] descended the steps slowly, struck across the Park, by the angle of the Rotunda, and stood on the brow of Chatham Street, towards the square. The Jews were as thick, with their gloomy whiskers, as blackberries; the air smelt of old coats and hats, and the side ways were glutted with dresses and over-coats and little, fat, greasy children. There were countrymen moving up and down the street, horribly harassed and perplexed, and every now and then falling into the hands of those fierce-whiskered Jews, carried into a gloomy cavern, and presently sent forth again, in a garment, coat or hat, or breeches in which he might dance and turn his partner, to boot.[5]

The imagery of this passage, built on the repetition of the word "gloomy," the stale, rank smells, the "fierce" whiskers, and the phrase, "thick . . . as blackberries," conveys a picture of a dreary but nevertheless striking environment isolated from those around it. The area has its own folkways—"a soft strain of the flute floated from a backroom . . . joined by a mellow, low whistle, which are, it is supposed, integral parts of speech in the dialect of Jewry." We perceive, therefore, the isolation of this community from the mainstream of the city's life and also have an implicit awareness that the environment which works on these people fosters their strangeness by its very isolation.

Not only does Mathews show contemporary scenes in his effort to evoke a sense of place, but he also shows how an area can be picturesque because of what it once was as well as what it now is. When Big Abel and the Little Manhattan pass a shoe store in front of which the owner and his clerk are hanging up a "Giant Boot," Lankey Fogle, the Little Manhattan, is prompted to speak of an old Indian village that used to stand on the very site of the shoe store. He recalls "dusty wigwams and council-fires, lit there, just where they stood, and trophies hung upon the trees" (21). By contrasting past and present here, Mathews reveals the banality of the contemporary, commercial world, particularly when seen in relation to its more heroic past. A great, ugly boot advertisement is not as poetic as Indian war trophies hanging from the trees—just as city streets are often less romantic than an unspoiled forest. Thus, when little that is striking exists in the scene, Mathews places it in the context of romance by linking it with a more picturesque past; at the same time, he indicates what is lacking in the present.

The present, Mathews wants his readers to remember, is not always so banal and tiresome. Often, it is quite charming and appealing. Walking alongside the East River, Big Abel and Lankey pass "lumberyards with cool, shady recesses: idle hay-bales sleeping out on the pier in the sun: stone-cutters: coalyards painting the neighborhoods about with a touch or two of their free brush" (27). Adding flair to the scene is a picturesque old riverman in a "weather-beaten boat" lying against the wharf. He is in "a faded tarpaulin with nankins faded to match; coatless, but with a blue cloth waist-coat of homespun texture" (27). Farther down the river, at New York Bay, they see a similar character, an old sea captain, the sight of whom conjures up the romance of faraway travel, a romance which is inescapably part of the New York City scene. He walks along close to the water, an "old sea-dog of a grizzled captain," sniffing the salty air and catching a "flavor of the oakum and the tar that lingers round about." Looking at him, one can glimpse "the thousand storms he knew of, off Bahamas and the Capes, and down the hot Gulf Stream" (40).

Even in the New York City market places, which other, less consciously "American," writers might find too banal for literary treatment, Mathews finds beauty and color. In such a market place Mrs. Saltus, a friend of Big Abel and Lankey, has her stand at which she works "within a world of greens, dewey from the fields, in baskets, in bundles, spread on a table before her, heaped about her on the ground." In her "rustling" speech, "sparkling eyes and waving motion," she "savors of the cornfield, the brook, and garden-life, where all these things took their growth" (34).

Mathews' observation of city life is more than a simple transcription of physical objects, for he is also receptive to the varied and subtle rhythms of the metropolis. His description of the city's waking up on a weekday morning captures the energy and excitement of the fast-paced urban life; and the short, ejaculatory sentences and phrases convey the excitement and hurry of the scene:

The city wide awake again! Nimble, serpent-eyed, fresh, how he bears the crest this Monday morning, as though he had got back somehow to his prime, without a thought of all his cares and crosses and riots! Clear and wide awake! Everybody abroad, with a new face born of Sunday! Everybody with a sprightly good-morrow! Everybody at a higher rate of speed! People coming in from the Islands, from Jersey, from down the Bay, ripe for new traffic on the keenest edge! The cartmen hurrying to the wharves in clean frocks, collars even, snow-white, twinkling among the whispers of omnibus-drivers.

Up Broadway? "Right-up! Right-up!" This was the cry, passing the Bowling Green. (46)

He presents, however, a slower-paced rhythm of life in the slums: "Old houses all the way; with all the doors open, all the casements shattered, all the chimneys broken-cornered . . . meagre, yellow, long-necked bottles and red curtains, at windows, without number; crazy balconies overhanging the way, with idle women leaning over, and looking up and down the street; then about the doorways, on the ground, heavy fellows in roundabouts and flat-rimmed hats, loitering, with no sign of business or employment, past, present, or to come, to be read of anywhere in all their idle limbs or empty looks" (56). In such a dismal scene as this, Mathews has found and conveyed some aspects which are picturesque. More importantly, he has put before his readers a picture of an American social blight which all too many might have comfortably ignored.

In *Big Abel and the Little Manhattan* Mathews shows us that the American city can be used as subject matter for literature. Some aspects of city life are romantic; others are strange; and some, perhaps, are banal and ugly. But these blighted areas should not be overlooked since they are tinged with historical associations and since, above all, they are there, part of our lives, and, to some extent, a determining factor in them. Thus, the rapid rate of material progress makes the Indian, as in the case of the Little Manhattan, a marginal character in the American scene; and isolation keeps the Jews of Chatham Street strange and vulgar. Moreover, the slums of the big city perpetuate themselves, breeding more slum dwellers and worse hovels. These are all aspects of American life which the national authors must bring home to their readers by establishing a sense of place.

In 1853, Mathews' *A Pen-and-Ink Panorama of New York City* reveals his continuing effort to make Americans aware of their environment. In his preface to this work, he states that he has "attempted to paint a home picture"; and he invites us to a "panoramic exhibition" in which he will unroll before us "the streets and characters of a great city" that he has studied from his boyhood, and "each high-way and by-way of which" he claims to know as familiarly "as the dog-eared pages of Robinson Crusoe or the Pilgrim's Progress." He asks indulgence when he loiters "even at a penny show" or pauses to meditate by "an ancient lamp-post," and he asks his readers not to despise the "simple, homespun dresses" in which some of his characters may appear.[6]

From the tenor of this introduction, we understand that Mathews is putting New York City, in all its varied guises, on exhibit in order to call attention to its real people and to their way of life. This intent is in keeping with his continued aim to make Americans aware of all the facets of their national life because, to a great extent, as we have observed, a man is what his country is. Moreover, not only national nature but human nature in general is revealed in the particular. In this vein, Mathews says, "human nature is very nearly the same, whether under the toga, worn with so much dignity by the Roman Senators, as we see on the stage, or under the dress coat made by Mr. Snip-Snap, the Broadway or Bowery tailor" (8).

The method through which Mathews attempts to depict national nature and, by extension, human nature, through his colorful representation of the American scene, is described by James Callow in his *Kindred Spirits,* a study of the relations between early nine-

teenth-century New York City writers and their painter counterparts. Callow, who sees Mathews as using the standard painter's
technique of panoramic perspective, calls *A Pen-and-Ink Panorama* "an extremely clever adaptation of the moving panorama
for literary purposes ... designed to give its readers the feeling
that they were actually present at the showing of a mid-century
panorama." This panoramic perspective achieves several ends. It
attains drama and excitement by placing the observer in an unusual
position. Perhaps even more importantly, with regard to Mathews'
aims, the panorama reflects the notion that America is vast beyond
exhaustion, a place of horizons without limit.[7] Consequently, it
seems that through the very largeness of Mathews' scope here, as he
takes all New York City as his province and attempts to capture it
for a moving, panoramic view, he imposes a powerful sense of place
upon his readers. The rapidly shifting scenes, presented without
any real narrative thread other than the narrator's supposed walk
about the city, demand all our attention; and, therefore, we must
deal with their reality itself, not with some plot for which setting is
a vehicle or a means of imposing order on the action.

Mathews' panorama is one of constantly shifting perspectives.
In his first section, "Walk Preliminary," he speaks of seeing New
York City at dawn, a time at which he has never before viewed it;
and he claims that he scarcely knows himself to be in New York.
The emptiness and quiet of the streets make everything seem strange
and "somewhat fantastical"—"the horses in the early omnibuses
I regarded as toys; and the drivers, up there, as a sort of mandarins
or queer kind of ghosts."[8] Although he sees this experience as a
highly romantic one, he urges us to remember that he has merely
been looking on commonplace things with a new perspective. Taken
for granted, they are nothing; but, paid attention to, they repay
with wonder. This potential sense of wonder is not peculiar to dawn;
indeed, it can be attained at midday on Broadway, if one is ob-
servant and receptive; for the viewer's state of mind is all-important.
In this connection, Mathews states: "By familiarity we lose the
sense of objects about us—they cease to be men, houses, streets,
and become mere material forms—differing a little in height, color,
or shape, but having no appreciable character or distinguishable-
ness, one from another" (12).

Aware that too much familiarity breeds ignorance, Mathews takes a fresh look at New York's "Main Street," Broadway. The street, itself, says Mathews, is not distinctive: "Broadway cannot claim a single peculiarity for itself. There is not a single feature by which you can define it—no one quality by which it is distinguishable from the commonest street" (32). This lack of distinction is particularly curious because Broadway is "the mighty medium for the exhibition of all that is singular and eccentric"; for it is the place for parades, receptions for heroes, ... exhibits from far-off lands," and so forth. However, Mathews does find one aspect of its essential nature in the masses that frequent it on Sunday. For them, the area is a "test of respectability":

> For real life and the display of numbers, Broadway is in full force through Sunday, and with an increased power on Sunday evening. It is then that the nice dressing of New Yorkers is to be seen in the highest perfection—a solid mass from Grace Church to the Battery—a perfect Mississippi, with a double current up and down, of glossy broadcloth and unblemished De-Laines. An army on the march to battle could not move with stricter precision—a procession of monks and nuns bound convent-ward, with more sacred gravity. New York in Broadway, on that day, makes a mighty sacrifice to solemnity, requiting itself a little in the evening by stepping aside into the shops and gardens, and revelling in innumerable ice-creams. (35)

Mathews' sarcastic tone in this passage, as he speaks solemnly of "sacred gravity," conveys his scorn for these pompous fortunate who ostentatiously parade about, displaying their good luck. The stiff, pretentious atmosphere of the procession is described when Mathews speaks of the practice of socially "cutting" an acquaintance: "if you are in doubt about yourself ... if your hat is rusty or your coat 'going,' if you have been paragraphed as having failed ... shun Broadway as you would a fire"; for the luckless are shunned by their former friends (36). In this Broadway vignette, then, Mathews has evoked the sense of one more place for his readers and has depicted a facet of the American mentality.

Another aspect of the American scene and another facet of the American mentality are described by Mathews as he walks through the Bowery and wonders whether life is happier in these democratic environs or in the aristocratic sections of Broadway. This question he cannot resolve, but he can describe some of the differences between the two ways of life. Broadway has "more show than substance"; the Bowery is a world of essentials, a bit coarse perhaps, but a place where reality counts for more than ornamentation. Unlike Broadway denizens, the people of the Bowery "have, all of them, an appearance as if they had got up of a sudden and dressed in a hurry" (131); but one exception to the Bowery utilitarian rule is the "dandy." Mathews, ever on the watch for the picturesque, describes this phenomenon carefully, so that a colorful piece of American scenery will not go unnoticed. He states that "the style of this gentleman's costume is startling and extraordinary":

Blazing colors—stark staring blue for coat, brick red for waistcoat, breeches with a portentous green stripe, hat brushed up to the highest gloss, shiny as a new kettle—he rolls down the Bowery a perfect Meteor, before whose slightest scintillation a Broadway exquisite would dwindle to undistinguishable nothingness. The Broadway dandy dresses snug and small, reducing his person by stays and pulleys, close fitting coats, pants, vests, and gloves. The Bowery dandy would impress you with an idea of largeness, strength; he swells his chest, makes broad the brim of his hat, the skirts of his coat—cuts close his hair, which conveys a notion of vigor—and as for gloves, his muscular, broad hand speaks for itself—he has never been known to wear them. (131–32)

Such detailed and appreciative description of New York City types, with an awareness of the excitement and atmosphere of energy which they generated, would reach its fullest expression two years later in Whitman's *Leaves of Grass;* but Mathews, almost alone among his contemporaries, was paying attention to these local scenes for the twenty years immediately preceding *Leaves of Grass.*

From Broadway and Bowery types, Mathews turns to a remarkable individual in his chapter "An Authentic Account of P. T. Barnum Esq." He believes that Barnum fulfills an inevitable community need: he supplies the public with the diversions and conversational material necessary to its emotional well-being. Mathews treats Barnum as New York City's own culture hero who plays a role for the metropolis similar to that played by Davy Crockett or Mike Fink for the frontier. Like them, he is the great showman, except that he moves in a more consciously theatrical milieu than they do. Mathews, who chronicles Barnum's fantastic rise to success, appears to take all the pleasure of an old southwestern raconteur-humorist in recounting Barnum's clever swindles, such as the one in which he, traveling through the back country of western

Kentucky, came upon an old black woman, "and with a decision strongly characteristic of the man ... promptly made up his mind to two points, that she was about one hundred and fifty years old, and had been the nurse of Washington. Being clear on these two points himself, his next step was to satisfy the public." Mathews describes the pains that Barnum took to do so: first, he bought the slave; second, he produced an old parchment bill of sale which, supposedly, was proof that the father of George Washington had bought her. This parchment, of course, had been suitably soaked in tobacco juice and smoked over a slow fire in order to give it the necessary appearance of great antiquity. To heighten the effect, Barnum hired a small boy to open and fold the parchment continually, so as to convey the idea of its having been handled frequently in its century of existence (46–47).

As a result of these endeavors Barnum was hailed as a great public benefactor; but, as Mathews states, this benefaction did not prevent him from taking in "large sums of money at the doors of all the public exhibitions where the venerable Joyce [the Negro woman] appeared." She held edifying conversations on religion with learned divines, and her talks with scientists satisfied her that she was somewhere about one hundred and fifty years old. When she died, the postmortem by an "eminent surgeon" bore out Barnum's claims; the old slave must have been at least sixty (48). From this gambit, Barnum acquired the necessary reputation to go on to greater things, which are also recounted by Mathews in order to provide a picture of an authentic American folk hero and again to exhibit another colorful aspect of the actual national experience—with the implicit message being that other American writers ought to take advantage of the same fertile field of subject matter which he himself is harvesting.

In his panoramic picture of New York City Mathews does not ignore the daily lives of characters who had not appeared often in American literature heretofore. Consequently, he exhibits the late "Little Trappan," the attendant in the newspaper room of the New York Society Library. A man of no note whatever except in his own eyes, his eccentric sense of self-importance made him memorable to all who ever came into contact with him. An extremely officious man, he often might ask aloud, "Why the devil gentleman couldn't conduct themselves *as* gentlemen, and keep their legs off the tables!" (59). Moreover, he carried on a constant and, in his mind, epic struggle against the insects which were wont to invade the library; and he kept a memento box in which he exhibited his little trophies. Mathews describes the heroic spirit in which Little Trappan conducted his greatest quest in this insect hunt:

> There was a great bug, of the roach species, often to be seen about the place—a hideously ill-favored and ill-mannered monster—which with a preternatural activity seemed to possess the library in every direction— sometimes on desk, sometimes on ladder, tumbling and rolling about the floor—and perpetually, with a sort of brutish instinct of spite, throwing himself in the old man's way, and continually thwarting his plans. And he was never, with all his activity and intensity of purpose, able to capture the great bug and *stick a pin through him* as he desired. This, we think, wore upon the old man and finally shortened his days. (62)

This poor, insignificant librarian had a "burning and longing hope" to found a library which would be "in some measure worthy of the great city of New York." For ten years he spent all his spare money acquiring books (usually being overcharged); and, by his death, he had amassed three hundred, which he willed to the library.

Mathews gives us this account of Little Trappan not because he was a success or a hero, but because he existed and dreamed. For like reasons Arthur Miller presented the story of Willy Loman, another little man motivated by a dream he could not attain. Little Trappan, Willy Loman, and millions like them are part of the American scene and ought not to be neglected, and Cornelius Mathews played a part in bringing their world into American literature.

Similarly, part of the city and, hence, the national environment, is the fireman, whom Mathews sees as a latter-day Chevalier, a selfless "knight errant" encased in leathern cap, red-flannel shirt, turned-up trousers and heavy boots, rushing forth on foot, "to do execution, without hire or reward, on that fiery dragon Combustion itself" (94). Mathews describes the rivalries, engine races, feuds, and riotous battles between the various proud fire companies; but he believes that the good these colorful characters perform more than outweighs their mischief, both in terms of the life and property that they save and in terms of the dash and excitement that they add to the New York scene.

A less exciting part, though, of metropolitan life is the world of the seamstress. Describing her daily routine, Mathews, in a tone of moral outrage, attacks the drudgery that many Americans have to bear. He reports that she rises at dawn; eats a quick, sparse breakfast; and then leaves for a sweatshop, carrying a load of clothes "to break the back of a small mule." As she walks, she faces an important decision: can she afford the six pence for an omnibus ride, and, if so, shall she take it downtown or up, "for remember she is to come back freighted with an equal weight of luggage from the shop" (115). When Mathews follows her to the shop, he observes the miserable conditions under which she labors; and he can predict no future comfort for her, unless she, as many of her co-workers have already done, gives up her job and lapses into prostitution.

Another lower-class figure whom Mathews stops to consider in his walk around New York is the newsboy. In his picture of the newsboy's life, he not only calls attention to the boy's social and economic deprivation but also describes a milieu which is peculiar to New York. Mathews declares, in fact, that "the genuine newsboy, in his full development and activity, . . . does not exist, except in New York." The Philadelphia newsboy hawks his papers with an unfortunate "slow-and-easy, deliberate sing-song which inspires you with anything but a desire to read the news" (182). However, in New York, "the quick, snapping cry, uttered while under a full run, and trailing along like the smoke of a steam-pipe with the boat at the top of her speed," communicates a state of excitement which pervades the whole city. Mathews describes the newsboy as "the lemon in the tumbler of everyday life, making it pungent and smart with a flavor" (183). Continuing his effort to provide the details necessary to give the reader the full picture of the local scene, Mathews reports on the state of the newsboy's clothing; and he finds that "he does not affect the latest fashions." He claims that no "legitimate" newsboy has ever been seen in a whole suit; "the uniform of his craft is a slouched cloth cap, dilapidated roundabout and breeches, no shoes nor stockings, and a dirty face with hands to match" (184). The newsboy's demeanor matches his physical appearance: he is continually swearing, drinking, fighting, and generally rousting about; and he is never without dice or cards in his pockets.

One of the newsboy's habitual treats is a trip to the theater, and

Mathews' description of the newsboy in attendance at a play not only portrays a piece of New York night life but also satirizes the condition of much of the contemporary theater; for the producers that cater to the newsboy mentality are those who are keeping serious American drama from developing. Unfortunately, as one might expect, the newsboy has little appreciation of the subtle; he admires "thunder and lightning, long-swords, casques, and black-whiskered villains, with mysterious exits and entrances in preference to everyday life." Mathews relates the extent to which the New York theater panders to such tastes: "There was a Mr. Kirby . . . who had great favor among the newsboys by his convulsive, awful manner of yielding up the ghost on the stage. . . . The newsboys, however, held the late Mr. Kirby to a strict account. If he omitted a single groan or distortion of feature, there was a general howl of disapprobation through the pit, and that actor was compelled, more than once, to go through a death struggle a second and even third time, till it satisfied the high requirements of these young censors" (188). Mathews wants to impress upon his readers that, comical as such circumstances may be, they are detrimental to the cause of American literature and, therefore, to America itself.

For the last segment in his panoramic depiction of New York, Mathews climbs to a high perch to get a "Birds-Eye View of New York from Latting's Observatory." From here, he can observe the natural panorama of the great city and its environs:

As the sun unrolls the wide veil [of haze] there comes out more of the great city, the two rivers, the East and the North, then the suburbs: Brooklyn, near by, rising on its heights: New Jersey, with its great factory chimney: Hoboken, with its green walks: Williamsburgh, with its countless little cottages: then in the Bay, the Islands, Governor's, with its dark stone fort: Gibbet's, (where the pirates are hung): Staten Island, with ridgy back: villages dropped along the shore: Paterson, with the Falls scarcely visible. . . .

One thing, however, and above all, you are clearly sensible of at that great height—you feel it, if you do not see it—a universal movement of all the inland country toward New York as its centre: everything by an irresistable impulse and momentum, driving or driven on towards the city. . . . The birds that pass, as they often do, at this starry height, cannot with all their strength of wing fly to where New York is not a permanent idea, affecting the business and conduct of men. (204–9)

Mathews tends to see New York as the embodiment of all the energy and power of a materially thriving nation. However, in using New York and its surrounding environs, in *The Motley Book, Big Abel and the Little Manhattan,* and *A Pen-and-Ink Panorama of New York City,* as an epitome of the whole American scene, Mathews is not merely sounding hymns of praise to the growing country; for material progress and expansive energy are not enough. If one is to be truly American, he must have a living knowledge of his national scene; its people and their way of life must be familiar to him. It is this kind of knowledge which Mathews tries to provide in these works as he functions as a kind of national recorder by transcribing local scenes (often so local as to be effectually out of the way and overlooked). This function Emerson said should be a chief aim of the American poet; and like Walt Whitman, Mathews, the democrat, responded to the national need.

CHAPTER 5

Values and Manners on the American Scene

I *Observer of the American Market Place*

FOR the American writer concerned about the welfare of his nation a description of its scenery and more picturesque characters and customs cannot be enough; he must go deeper in his examination of the national experience. Consequently, Cornelius Mathews tried not only to explore the customs of his compatriots but to examine and describe their values—the things they believed in, the goals they tried to attain, and the feelings they had for their country. Mathews was certainly not alone in his concern for American values; for, by the mid-nineteenth century, Hawthorne and Melville were exploring the American psyche and describing what they uncovered. However, where these two were dealing mainly with the nature of the human heart and with the problems of man's confrontation with the ultimate reality, Mathews was more concerned with man as a social animal, and he presents fictionally much of what Emerson saw when he wrote about the American market place. Thus, in several sketches of *The Motley Book*, in *Moneypenny*, *Chanticleer*, and *False Pretences*, Mathews fully describes the situation which Emerson summarized when he wrote that "things are in the saddle and ride mankind." Indeed, in these words, Mathews carries out the function that another American moralist, James Fenimore Cooper, took upon himself in *Home as Found*—that of serving as a social commentator who attempts to recall foolish or pernicious Americans to the standards of rectitude and the more seemly, noble, and democratic demeanor of their forebears.

As early as the late 1830's, in his first published works, Mathews is concerned about an American sense of values which has gone awry. In a satirical sketch in *The Motley Book* entitled "The N. A. Society for Imposture" he attacks the fraudulent practices of all too many Americans who, either as merchants or professional men, are in positions of public trust. In this sketch, a society of charlatans has gathered for their annual meeting in which they are given a report on how the great cause of imposture is faring across the nation. We hear of "no less than twelve thousand common ten dollar, red shawls" sold at twenty-five dollars apiece as "actual merinos" and of two hundred and fifty pieces of "sky-blue home-spun" having been disposed of as "sea-green broadcloth by the proper arrangement of the light" in clothing stores. Pleasant news, also, is that the fashions they encourage, which call for shorter clothes, are catching on with the public, thus saving the merchants the money for extra cloth.[1]

Similarly, the society is happy to note that there has been a vast increase in the numbers of physicians and lawyers, for this "augurs the most favorable results to the cause": "Whatever can be done to promote its advancement by administering wrong medicines and improper advice, by purging, as it were, the system and the pocket, and by fabricating respectable and not too moderate bills of costs and charges, will . . . be done by the efficient and important auxiliaries to whom they have alluded. The number of mortgages galloped into foreclosure, of consumptive patients to whom stiff cathartics have been administered and of children who have been physicked indiscriminately without reference to the disease, is truly cheering and encouraging to your Board" (130).

An even more outrageous violation of the public trust is per-petrated by the religious leaders depicted in *The Motley Book* tale, "Parson Huckins' First Appearance," which satirizes the perversion of religion into something hateful and dishonest. The simple faith and virtues are gone and have been replaced by pre-tense and dishonesty. Thus, the smug Parson Huckins has been selected for his position merely because of his fine physical appear-ance and ringing voice, and his congregation admires him for such evidence of his zeal as his ability to slam his hand down on the pul-pit over a hundred times in the course of his sermon (177). The fine picture of courage and morality which Huckins presents is a fraud, however, for he caters to a vicious and powerful deacon (who knows of a hidden crime in the minister's past) by preaching a religion in which all are condemned to hell except for the handful of chosen American Protestants who make up the influential portion of Huckins' congregation. Furthermore, this would-be spiritual guide supplements his salary by swearing false affidavits for incompetent physicians and corrupt politicians (180). Although Huckins, of course, does not represent all ministers and although his church is not typical of all American churches, Mathews is obviously reacting through this story against what he sees as manifestations of a breakdown in religious values.

II   *The Gold Standard:* Moneypenny

More sweeping in its picture of a nation whose sense of values has become warped is *Moneypenny, or, the Heart of the World. A Romance of the Present Day* (1849). In this novel Mathews explicitly emphasizes, for the first time, the polarity which he sees existing in America between the rural way of life and its counterpart in the cities. He tends to identify rural areas with the virtues that led to the founding of the nation and that have continued to make it great, and he uses these virtues as a standard against which all actions and modes of behavior are measured. City life is usually presented as an aberrant departure from the standard. Unfortunately, though, America, as Mathews observes it, is fast becoming urban-oriented, and the older virtues, holding on in ever more isolated rural areas, are being forgotten by large numbers of Americans.

The importance of *Moneypenny*, then, resides largely in its incisive commentary on American values and manners; for, as is often the case with Mathews' work, the plot holds scant interest, being little more than the conventional story of a search for a lost son. Job Moneypenny, a kind, ingenuous, small-town merchant, accompanied by one Pythagoras Bunker who, like Parson Adams in Fielding's *Joseph Andrews,* wrongly fancies himself a sophisticate, leaves his rural home in upstate New York to go to the big city to find his lost son, mysteriously kidnapped many years before. The search is complicated, however, by a revenge-seeking illegitimate son, Pierce, who, not knowing that Moneypenny is his father, is under the delusion that Moneypenny has defrauded him of an inheritance left by the man that Pierce mistakenly believes is his grandfather. The facts, though, are that Moneypenny was the sole support of this man and that there is no inheritance. Pierce and a whole crew of sordid confederates mean to keep Moneypenny from finding his legitimate younger son, to blackmail him, and, perhaps, to kill him. More importantly, Moneypenny's efforts are complicated by the complex web of evil he stumbles into when he enters New York City. The city itself is a diseased environment, and those who enter it run the risk of becoming infected or of becoming in other ways victims. To a great extent, Pierce and his compatriots not only add to the metropolis' corruption but also exemplify it.

Ultimately, this work's value as social commentary derives from its depiction of the confrontation of a rural code of values and customs with those of the large city, a confrontation which involves an unsuspecting character's initiation into a firsthand knowledge of evil. This theme, does not, of course, begin in American literature with Mathews; for Charles Brockden Brown depicted it with a good deal of success in *Arthur Mervin,* while Melville touched on it in *Redburn* in the same year as *Moneypenny* and was to take it up again, a few years later, at greater length, in *Pierre.* However, Brown and Melville seem to be describing evil per se, with its transcendental implications, where Mathews deals with it merely in its social guises of inequity, avarice, and ostentation. Furthermore, this theme of initiation into knowledge of evil can even be glimpsed in Seba Smith's "Jack Downing" letters, although in a comic vein. Mathews, who mixes farce, satire, and melodrama, provides a fuller depiction than do any of these writers of the manners and values of the big city.

In the preface to *Moneypenny,* Mathews, who states his aims as a social observer in this work, claims that his novel is "intended to illustrate the various classes of which our active and miscellaneous society is composed." He then declares archly: "That he [the author] has endeavored to present one of the leading persons of his story as a man of Christian spirit (though subject to the frailties of humanity), a reader of his Bible, and relying on the great providence of God—in the midst of many characters busily engaged with fashion or folly, among scenes of vice, exhibitions of the humors of (so-called) law, and the gayeties of high life—will he trusts, make it none the less acceptable to either of these numerous classes of readers."[2]

We first see Job Moneypenny—a decent man who, Mathews believes, may be too decent to be a palatable hero for novel readers— in his comfortable home in Greenbush, a peaceful village far from the noise and strife of the city. Satirizing the urban point of view,

Mathews attacks the little town for being inhabited by "silly people who mainly busy themselves in digging the earth and shaking apple trees in autumn" (26). Moreover, the town is so "ridiculous" that it has "neither doctor, lawyer, nor divine, for the foolish fellow who read the Bible and talked plain English to the village folks on Sunday was not worthy of that name" (25). In the midst of this "silly" little village sits the Moneypenny home, into which we are introduced at breakfast time. This scene represents the best aspects of the American tradition: unassuming friendliness and virtue, as manifested by a large country breakfast, pictured in loving detail; a comfortable room; and kind, homespun people. Job Moneypenny is described as a small-town Samaritan whose life has been dedicated to helping others, and, indeed, even his Negro servants lament "Uncle Job's" leaving for New York. He is to be accompanied by Pythagoras Bunker, another guileless, small-town type, whose experience in the metropolis ten years before, when he was mercilessly and repeatedly fleeced, leads him to believe that he is an experienced hand who can protect Job from the city's pitfalls; with bravado Bunker declares, as he will throughout his misadventures, "I'll see that everything goes right. I wasn't in York ten years ago for nothing" (28). However, even by their physical appearance, it is apparent that these two men are no match for the deviousness of the city. Mathews frequently characterizes people by the clothes they wear; and the simple, unfashionable apparel of rural cut worn by the two travelers proclaims their vulnerability.

Thus, with even their appearance advertising their credulousness, the two unsophisticates depart for the big city. Mathews uses their adventures there as a vehicle for examining the manners, habits, fashions, and, underlying all of these, the morality of the New Yorkers, whom he sees as representative of a type that is becoming increasingly prevalent throughout the country as such peaceful byways as Greenbush become invaded by the new, mid-nineteenth-century American mentality. Through depiction of the reactions of Moneypenny and Bunker to the city and its reception of them, Mathews presents the clash of two American ways of life—the rural, with its traditional values and customs, and the increasingly prevalent urban one, with its new emphasis on material wealth and grand appearance.

The steamboat trip down the Hudson River and into the city not only serves as a transitional device, giving Moneypenny his first view of urban life, but also symbolizes the country's rush toward the power and wealth that the city represents. Merely boarding the steamboat brings Job Moneypenny, representative of the social ideals of an earlier America, into a new, bewildering world of which he knows little. In contemplating the steamboat he reminds one of Henry Adams, another American who, years later, looked at a modern machine and saw a strange new world which frightened and perplexed him. Moneypenny sees crowded on the deck of the steamboat more people than there are in the whole of his village, more than he has ever seen in one place before; and he thinks, longingly, of the fields and woods of Greenbush, "when old Autumn had been busiest with his brush" (33).

On board the steamboat, Moneypenny meets people whose way of life is so alien to him that he is unable to perceive how obviously foolish and corrupt they are. He falls in with the Joneses, a wealthy family returning from a vacation at Saratoga Springs. Mrs. Jones is a New York society matron whose major concern in life is to be in fashion and who advertises her claims to social status by giving lavish parties. Her son, a worthless fop—scornfully referred to by Mathews as "the hope of the Nineteenth Century" (35)—derives his lack of character directly from his mother's strange priority of values. Again delineating an individual through his clothing, Mathews describes the costume of the Jones son. His red hair, vigorously frizzed, is neatly set off by a "checkerboard straw hat, with a flying ribbon, a striped shirt, check pants, check gaiters and an olive coat, with long gaping pockets, bobbed off just above the buttons, with a small pole constantly sticking out of one of them, which he kept poking into people's faces all about the boat" (35). Even more ridiculous than the boy's outfit is the knowing air which he consciously exudes. Only nineteen years old, this spoiled, decadent child has a bearing that seems to ask, "can you tell me where I haven't been and what I don't know?" He seems to tell passersby, "I've seen more, done more, sworn more, said more than many men of seventy" (35).

Young Jones's rush to worldly experience typifies the hurried pace of the modern world, one which has completely bypassed such backwater spots as Greenbush. Fittingly enough, Job is ushered into this fast-paced world by a steamboat race down the Hudson; the speed with which the *Overshot* and a rival boat hurtle toward New York symbolizes the national situation, which is that of an increasingly materialistic and industrial society hurrying toward some new destiny to which it has given little thought—all that matters is the chase. While excited by the rush of progress, Americans tend to forget their traditional values and their ties with the past and the land:

There was no time to stop and consider that here at Kingston, which they were passing like an arrow, two tories were hung for treason during the Revolutionary War, that the first Constitution of the state was adopted here in '77, and that Judge Hasbroeck, still living, can tell you all about both events. Speed! Speed! If there is any virtue in steam it shall be tried today! And yet, could we stop, how fair is the river here, with its low meadow-banks, its woodland backgrounds, its quiet little creeks and inlets—but no—on!—on! (37)

The human values are forgotten; the steamboats neglect to pick up their passengers; and a frightened old woman, who screams that she wants to be put ashore, is viewed by the other passengers as if they would like to lynch her (39).

Near the end of the race, Job sees the city ahead, lying in the twilight, "large, dark and massive." He regards it fearfully, "as though it were some beast of prey crouching on the river-bank in the dark"; and, seeing innumerable lights "glaring forth," he has a "strange apprehension of evil approaching" (42). Intimidated by the immensity of the city, Job wonders how he can even hope to succeed in his quest. On the other hand, the less perceptive Pythagoras chortingly declares, "there's old York, I know it as well as I know the palm of my own hand." Less reassuring, though, is the end of the race; for the rival steamboat bursts its boiler and sinks in New York harbor, providing an ominous beginning for Job's venture.

On landing at the city, Job and Pythagoras immediately reveal themselves as at variance with the tempo and manners of city life. Job rescues a little newsboy from a beating and then must pay off the police in order to avoid arrest for his decent action. A few blocks later, a fire company comes charging by; and Pythagoras, not experienced enough to get out of the way, gets tangled up in the hoses and is dragged down the street. Even when they are finally off the streets and established at a hotel, their habits are out of place in this New York City context. Thus, when arising for his first morning in New York and carefully washing, shaving, and dressing "like a Christian man," Job is startled to hear a loud moaning that grows and swells to "something like the bellowing of a bull" (54). However, this is merely the gong for breakfast.

Walking leisurely downstairs, as he was wont to do at home, Moneypenny comes upon a huge room filled with eaters and servers "rushing hither and thither like madmen"; all are making "such a clatter and concerto of noises, metallic, earthen, human, all commingled, as no musician of the utmost skill—no orchestra of musicians—could ever hope to accomplish" (54). Entering the dining room, he soon makes himself thoroughly objectionable to the corps of waiters in attendance; for he chooses to eat slowly, and even to ask for seconds, to the extent of taking a full half-hour for breakfast and finishing in an empty dining room. This, of course, is not the New Yorker's manner of eating, which is to start early, bolt down food in a moment, and dash off. Pythagoras, thinking himself the prototype city swell, finds Job "very much to blame in the extraordinary course he pursued" (55) and, later, is appalled by Moneypenny's complaints about the extremely meager dinners they receive at a "select" boardinghouse to which they have been steered by Pierce, who has "befriended" them.

The lack of concern for the individual which we see both at the hotel and the boardinghouse is no more than a manifestation of the city's general disregard of man's basic humanity. Rather than provide hospitality or help as the earlier, rural America might, the New York residents usually ignore or take advantage of the helpless. Consequently, when Pythagoras goes to an Intelligence (or Employment) Office, thinking that it provides information, and asks the manager for help in finding a lost child, the manager lies and says he can help him, for a fee, of course. Thus begins Pythagoras' series of visits to the office, in which he is inevitably told that the child has not yet been found. However, in order to keep taking his money, the manager continually holds out hope for the lost Felix; and at each visit he tells Pythagoras that this time he thinks he can accommodate him with a son for Mr. Moneypenny. The son is to be culled from the group of young men sitting in the room, seeking jobs: "turf-trotting Irishmen, heavy-footed Dutchmen, long-haired Norwegians, dapper Frenchmen, talking all the languages of the known globe" (73). Pythagoras, impressed by the office's efforts, must ruefully, and almost guiltily, confess that Felix is none of these. On hearing this, the diligent manager is "greatly cast down." However, he is not too cast down to ask Pythagoras to call again tomorrow, as Pythagoras assuredly will.

Unable to depend on others for help, Moneypenny and Bunker must rely on their own efforts; and they wander the city themselves, remaining receptive to any clue which might be forthcoming. By following them as they roam about the city, the book takes on a loosely plotted, episodic structure through which Mathews is able to depict many aspects of New York City life which might have gone untreated had he used a more tightly constructed plot. Thus, to some extent, we have here a fictional forerunner of Mathews' sweeping view of New York in *A Pen-and-Ink Panorama*.

The large scope of action made possible by Mathews' episodic structure enables him to observe the manners and values of all strata of New York society, from the newsboys' level to that of the aristocracy, as represented by the Jones family. The acquaintance that Moneypenny made with this family while on the steamboat gains him an invitation to a gala ball at their house, which gives Mathews (and the readers) entrée into the world of the fashionable New York socialites, one of waste and foolish extravagance. Its values are such that Jones, Jr., spends an entire afternoon bestowing on his new mustache "all the tender solicitude an anxious mother bestows on her first born" (78); and, following these exertions, he joins his mother to have their hair curled by the latest of the eminent French hairdressers.

Finally, evening arrives and the brilliant entertainment begins. The party is attended by all the elite of New York, or, in other words, as Mathews presents it, by every fop, dandy, and status-seeking society matron of the city. It proves to be an event at which poor Moneypenny is totally out of place, for it is a function of a world far different from that of Greenbush; here all that matters is appearance, while Moneypenny was taught to value substance. Mathews describes the company as engaged in a deliberate scrutiny of each other's dresses in order to estimate the cost of "getting up," and "no sharp milliner, or calculating mantua-maker" could possibly provide as severe and comprehensive an examination as do these fine ladies.

At the height of the evening the orchestra suddenly breaks into "Hail the Chief" and in "marches, lounges, or sidles—for it is an elaborate compound of all these movements—Jones, Jr." (81). He is supported on one hand by Charley Ballard, Esq. (a con-man friend of Pierce's) and on the other by a pool-room hustler named Harry, who makes his livelihood off spoiled simpletons like Lafayette Jones, Jr. Moneypenny, in his simple clothes, sitting alone in a corner, thinks that young Jones would suffer immeasurably by contrast with Demus Hammersley, a swain of Greenbush, who is taller, "bigger in the girth, and has more hair." In short, in Money-penny's "foolish opinion," Demus, who could bring down an ox with his fist, is "more of a man in every way" (82). Indeed, Money-penny finds the whole evening's entertainment, despite its glare, motion, and talk, falling short of more pleasant evenings at home when he had seen "more fun and more fancy" at "many a quilt-ing, in many a farmer's wife's parlor with no other music than the whistling of Demus Hammersley and Bunker" (83). Even ice-cream pyramids and buildings of Charlotte-Russe cannot save the evening, in Moneypenny's estimation. To add to his displeasure is the card game he allows himself to get talked into—one in which he and young Jones are swindled out of a tidy sum by Pierce and Ballard.

Some days later, Mr. Moneypenny is again present at an enter-tainment given by the Jones family. This time it is a gala breakfast and art exhibit held for the benefit of a visiting English nobleman, Sir Bluster Ruggles. Mathews uses this entertainment as a means of attacking American obsequiousness before foreigners and their opinions and of satirizing what he conceives to be some of the more absurd trends in American art and criticism. In the figure of M. Leowulf Dekerdogge, "first violin to his gracious majesty the King of Norway," Mathews parodies the fake "artists" who, because they are foreigners, are taken up and catered to by status-seeking Americans. Mathews describes Dekerdogge's ostentatious and ridiculous manner of judging art and of becoming "inspired" by it:

He proceeded in his check pants, to leap about like a great frog, inspecting the walls. With an irrepressible galvanic movement, he passed from one painting to another, till he came to a mass of white and green, which passes in the popular eye for the Falls of Niagara, as seen from some point by somebody or other, and which brought him to a standstill. Three times he rolled his eyes about, and three times he lifted his eyes. Then he cried, "I have it!" and fell back to the fire again, where he stood, congratulating himself. (190)

Such comfort does not last long, however, for another foreign musician soon enters—a "second apparition, still wilder than the first, with more hair, a bigger check in his breeches, and his coat buttoned with fury to the throat." He cavorts around the room in a similar manner and concludes by shouting, "I have it" (191). An acrimonious debate ensues in which each artist claims that he "has" a Niagara symphony which will soon be presented before "the generous American public" (191). The assembled guests, except for Moneypenny, are suitably impressed, and the "artists" are ensured continued patronage.

Perhaps even more impressive to the guests than these accomplished artists is Captain Pool, an art critic and a special guest of the Joneses. Pool, a traveled gentleman, is a "fearful connoisseur" in paintings, who immediately glides about the rooms, with his great eyeglass in active service. Pool's standards of criticism, if not terribly explicit, are at least consistent. Underlying his theory of art is a philosophy whose power can never be ignored—snob appeal. When asked his opinion about one painting, he gives it his studied approbation, replying "an undoubted old master." He comes to another. "'A poor thing, sir,' said Captain Pool, with scorn on his lips, 'not an old master!'" Another painting is "almost equal to one of the old masters" (192).

Awesome as the exercise of this critical faculty is, it seems that the greatest social lion on the scene is the visiting Englishman, Sir Bluster Ruggles. The Americans at the exhibition are completely cowed by this little nobleman's mere presence. Moreover, they are ludicrously self-conscious, for they believe that Sir Bluster, like all foreigners in the United States, will, in time, publish a book of observations about Americans. Stung so often by bad notices of their country, and not self-reliant enough to ignore most of these comments for the ignorant tripe they often are, they observe the Englishman with apprehension:

"You see how he puts his hands under his coat-tails, and looks about: there's no doubt he's taking notes in his head this very minute!" ... The company looked on wondering. They all felt guilty of something or other, they didn't know what; and stood condemned and convicted of some heinous misdemeanor in presence of the terrible and majestic Sir Bluster! . . . They were now assured he was busy on a book on America; they already saw it issued from the London press; heard its dread thunders rolling across the Atlantic; and saw, as the fearful gust of Sir Bluster's denunciation swept the land, the whole numerous population of America bowed down in the dust in humiliation and conscious imbecility before the scourge of the remorseless Ruggles. (194)

However, these frightened sycophants believe that they will be able to please Sir Bluster with what is to be the *pièce de résistance* of the exhibition—the model for a national monument to George Washington. Mathews uses the occasion of its exhibition as a means of pointing out the miserable plight of the American artist in his own country, and, perhaps, at the same time, of satirizing Horatio Greenough's recent statue of Washington. Mr. Slack, the sculptor of the model, is forced to carry the monstrously heavy thing himself to the Jones home. On getting it there, his shabby clothes and his haggard, care-worn appearance are taken for those of a beggar or organ-grinder, and he is refused admission. Finally gaining entry, he is made to wrestle the sculpture into place, alone, with the indifferent help of one of the Jones family's black servants; and he is subjected to the additional indignity of hearing Captain Pool proclaim, before the piece is even uncrated, that it is "quite equal to the old masters."

Mathews' description of the model makes it evident that he is using it as a means of attacking the American public which forces its artists to imitate foreign modes. Painted an intense sky blue, the structure has fluted columns; and the artist stammers "piteously" that it is meant for a barn. However, his generous patron, Jones, Jr., will have none of this and grandly declares that "it's the Temple of Agriculture and it's devoted to Washington the farmer's son . . . you may call it a barn if you choose, but it's on the exact model of the Parthenon at Athens" (196). At the door of the Temple is a figure with light yellow trousers, a ruffled shirt, and pumps with silver buckles. Young Jones claims that it is "the boy Washington, feeding chickens; you'll notice they are not common fowls. They're bantams of the best English breed, to give elevation to the design, in place of the common barnyard poultry" (196).

There are representations of Washington at other stages of his career, all patterned after European models and all ludicrous. In one representation, his legs are "an exact copy of the Apollo Belvy at Rome"; in another, his cocked hat is "an exact copy after Marshal Turenne in the Louvre" (196). One pose which startles all the observers depicts Washington as a brawny man with his two arms raised "as if he was on the point of throwing a back-somerset." The artist is too embarrassed to explain this posture, but Jones, Jr., glibly asserts, "that's Washington taking his exercise, and strengthening his frame preparatory to entering on his arduous career, in the appropriate character of an athlete to the Olympic Games" (197). Inside the Temple, we see Washington "ascending the ladder, with a tunic about his body, and a helmet on his head." This, the patron announces, is "the immortal Washington on his way to assume the dignity of General-in-Chief of the American Forces, which was supposed, in the model, to be somewhere up-stairs" (197). One of the observers with some common sense de-clares, forthrightly, "Washington never wore such a rig as that." Jones answers, "We know that, but we intend this to be something classical, Colonel; in the real dress he wore, it would have been, you know, vulgar,—decidedly and devilish low" (197).

Finally, we see, on the roof of the Temple, Washington in a loin-cloth, and sprouting wings ready to take off. Sir Bluster asks, "what strange fowl have we here!" It is, of course, the apotheosis of Washington. All agree that the model is impressive, but Sir Bluster is insulted because the Duke of Wellington is not represented, "I'm dom'd if my old friend the Duke ben't as good a right to be there as them Roman fellows; and I'd like to know why he be left out" (198). His opinion, because he is British, carries great weight, and all immediately proclaim the work a miserable failure. Captain Pool confidently asserts the work is "not equal to the old masters"; and the artist, now contemptuously disavowed by Jones and his mother, is put out. The sympathetic Moneypenny speaks with the sculptor, who declares that poverty forced him to accept Jones's meager patronage and asinine advice, thus making the work a hopeless botch and a dishonor to Washington. Ashamed and angry, he smashes his model and rushes away.

The foolishness and corruption of high society are only part of a malaise affecting much of New York City life and permeating both the affluent and the poor. When all values are based on material possessions and grand appearance, virtue disappears. The

rich are not Cooper's responsible social leaders; the poor are not
Longfellow's simple, honest blacksmiths. In New York the decadence and the puerility of the rich are often matched by the mean-
ness and viciousness of the poor. Thus, we see Pierce's cohort,
Charley Ballard, who, rather than work, makes his way as a pick-
pocket and a con-man; and, like Melville's confidence man, he
wears a mourning crepe on his hat in order to take advantage of
those who befriend him and offer sympathy. He has no compunction
whatever about working for Pierce; but, when his boss's plot is
foiled, Ballard has a "reformation" and gains a pardon by testify-
ing against him.

Another of Pierce's helpmates is a prostitute named Sue, who
is not a courtesan with a heart of gold but a low, vicious woman,
whose tastes and values are a tawdry ape of those of New York's
high society, in itself a worshiper of the sham and the ugly. The
prostitute's way of life is illustrated by Mathews' picture of Sue sitting in her overlavish apartment, furnished in a manner revealing
pretensions to being in high fashion, and working, as any lady of
high tone might, on a dainty crayon sketch. The implicit ugliness
of this scene becomes blatant when she opens her mouth and de-
murely greets a caller; "Why, 'Gus, blast me, are you back again?"
(21). Sue's pretensions render her ridiculous; but, at the same time,
they create an atmosphere of sordidness and decadence which,
Mathews seems to hint, is a commentary on the American upper
class with its pretensions and, consequently, its own decadence.
Perhaps unduly lavish tastes led Sue into prostitution just as much
as did any social inequity; certainly the ostentatiously lavish tastes
of the American *nouveau riche* (and it seems that Mathews believes,
with just cause, that *all* wealthy Americans are *nouveau riche*)
have corrupted them and made them ridiculous. Ballard and Sue
are not isolated cases of poverty without honesty, for *Moneypenny*
is a panoramic view of pervasive dishonesty.

As Mathews takes us about town, we see poor slum boys beating
up other poor slum boys, shabby merchants defrauding even shab-
bier customers, and poverty-stricken thieves robbing the poverty-
stricken. As glimpsed in *Big Abel and the Little Manhattan,* life in
the slums is ugly and unpleasant. However, Mathews also provides
a picture of the way in which slum dwellers react to one another.
In the yard of a typical slum dwelling there is a "constant jostling

against each other of bare-footed and frouzy-haired women, going to and from the cistern." A perpetual controversy is kept up at the "common entrance . . . as to the rights and duties of the respective flights—for they class themselves by stairways" (100). Mathews describes man's absurd but seemingly innate need to set up arbitrary social distinctions, a need so strong that even slum dwellers exhibit it by aligning themselves according to the flights in their tenement building. The ugliness and the banality of the lives of these tenement poor are graphically depicted when Mathews shows one of the usual spats in progress: " 'Mrs. Macginnis had better look after her own. I'll take my Bible oath, she never put a drop on the stairs but what she spilled in fetching water.' 'Clean your own flight, you nasty beast.' 'You're always carrying stories to your man.' 'You mustn't say that of me, Widow Fogleheimer.' 'I will—and what's more, I'm the woman to back it up!' 'None of your Dutch sas!' 'It's better than English chops, any day of the year—that for you!' " (100).

Epitomizing the evil and viciousness of the lower depths in New York City is the villain of *Moneypenny,* Pierce. This blackguard never honestly confronts Moneypenny with the grievance he holds against him; instead, he attempts to rob and murder him. We have here no ambitious poor, no stout American yeoman who will make the American dream operative, but a skulking scoundrel. However, Mathews wants us to remember that Pierce is not entirely to blame for the evil path he has followed, that society had a large hand in his moral failure. In his cell, waiting to be hanged, Pierce is offered some money owed him, and he recoils, shouting, "I will never touch it again, nor look at it, if I can keep it from my sight" (251). He declares that it is money which has corrupted him: "If I had not been taught, as a poor broker's boy, by what I heard every day and every hour, that money was the god of the world; that to have it not was to be a worthless outcast in a generation of seekers of gold; that to have it was to be all that was good and enviable—if I had not been slighted by other boys and men because I was poor, inflamed by all I saw, and heard, and knew, to seek it in every channel, by every act of the strong hand and the subtle tongue, I should not have come to this!" (251).

Unfortunately, the reformers who would attempt to change the American code of values are, as Mathews sees them, unrealistic, ineffectual, self-delusive malcontents. One such malcontent, Miss

Melia Wright (perhaps modeled unflatteringly, on the controversial reformer, Frances Wright) is an unwilling spinster, who declares that marriage must be abolished if society is to improve. "Love," she claims, "is the most awful and abominable delusion that has ever scourged the human family." It is, she asserts, "through all ages the desolator!" Why must a "free spirit—a noble spirit" with "a soaring soul" be tied down to a "weak, helpless woman?" (108). In place of marriage she advocates a "common domicile" for two or three hundred people; in such an arrangement, Mathews hints, Miss Wright hopes to achieve the personal sexual gratification which is, though she will not admit it to herself, the fundamental goal toward which her reforms are aimed.

Perhaps a better means of effecting social amelioration would be through setting up a climate which is conducive to reform. However, the powerful daily newspapers, potentially the most effective instrument in mobilizing public support for such reform, are concerned only with the size of their profits. Consequently, instead of socially perceptive, crusading reporters, we see money-hungry sensation-seekers such as Dexter Hawley (perhaps modeled on Cooper's Steadfast Dodge), who, as first seen on the steamboat coming back from Saratoga Springs, is darting about "spasmodically, with a long wooden pencil in hand, and leaves, or slips of soiled paper sticking out of his coat-tail pocket. . . . Plunging his nose freely into this group and that," he speaks of the advantages of advertising—"the great secret of success in business is copious and unlimited advertising"—and, when he finds fault with the way he is treated on the boat, he threatens a dreadful exposure in the *Pipe* (34).

When next seen, Hawley is rushing into a tenement, hot on the trail of a story. He feverishly demands of one of the dwellers, "Is it true—is it so?" as he takes his soiled notebook from his hat. When asked what he means, he exasperatedly shouts, "the child! the child. . . . Good heavens! Don't you understand me—the Dutch child that fell from the fifth story, not five minutes ago—where is it? Can I get a sight of the corpse for a minute only? Have the 'Trumpet' people been here?" (104). Hawley seems terribly disappointed when he finds that, in fact, no child has been killed falling from a window. Such reporters, obviously, will do nothing to reshape the values of their countrymen; and their "soiled notebooks" are badges not only of their physical, but also their moral, shabbiness.

The editor of Hawley's paper, the *Organ Pipe,* is a Colonel Inkey, who loves to pontificate incoherently on the state of the world and then see his utterances in print. Other than using the paper as an outlet for his rantings and giving the public the sensational stories that it wants, Inkey cares little about the paper and its social responsibilites. This attitude filters down to his subordinates, who make certain not only that each news report is sensational but that it is one which does little to disturb the status quo. Thus, the newsboy, Teddy Larkins (promoted to reporter by Mr. Moneypenny when he buys a controlling interest in the paper) is reprimanded by the assistant editor, who, "pale with suppressed indignation," declares that Teddy must be careful because he speaks tenderly in one of his reports of a man who stole a loaf of bread, when of course, the man should be reviled as a wretch. Moreover, he declares, "when Mr. James appeared before the court yesterday, in the matter of the defalcation of fifty thousand dollars at the bank, you treat him like any common fellow, and as more of a thief than the other man." Teddy's answer, "well, isn't he?," as might be expected, provokes the assistant editor into a rage (202). Justice soon prevails, though, as Moneypenny makes Teddy the editor. Such occurrences as Teddy's promotion are assuredly rare, and Mathews is describing a situation in which the only mass medium available for public communication continually fails in its role.

In *Moneypenny,* then, Mathews' picture of American life, as manifested in its greatest city, is not a flattering one. Evil and folly are pervasive and tend inevitably to perpetuate themselves. However, he also provides an alternative to the crisis in social values and manners. This alternative resides in a return to the way of life of the earlier America, the way of life which gave birth to the nation. It is one based on simple virtue, benevolence, and an eschewal of the tawdry and materialistic. Such a way of life is embodied by Moneypenny, who in the process of finding his lost son (little Teddy Larkins, of course), does work some social change, such as reforming one newspaper, and dispensing charity to the deserving poor. Needless to say, Moneypenny is only one man; and, though he is richer than most, the values he represents are nonetheless valid and worthy of emulation. Furthermore, these values are not dead; they still exist here and there on the American scene, even amidst poverty; and, if fostered, they could, perhaps, reassert themselves on a national scale.

One of those few typifying the true American democrat, who still is part of American life, is butcher-boy Ike Williams, who steps in several times in the course of the novel to save Moneypenny from harm. Crophaired and "large-fisted," he hates affectation and cares only for honesty and fair play. When first met, he and his brindle bulldog, "General Zack Taylor," save Moneypenny from robbers set upon him by Pierce. Later, Ike selflessly aids Moneypenny in finding his lost son and indignantly refuses a reward. Such fundamental decency as Ike Williams shows hints that the average American has it in him to be a much better man than he usually reveals. In order to exhibit this capability, he must return to the code of values and way of life on which this country was based.

Thus, in *Moneypenny* Mathews has effected a salient and compelling commentary on modern American manners and values as reflected on many levels of New York City life. His manner of pointing up folly, corruption, and evil by juxtaposing them against a picture of a better life as manifested by Job Moneypenny and Ike Williams, one based on traditional American values, makes for some rather successful dramatic contrasts. While the puerility of the plot often makes *Moneypenny* tedious and cliché-ridden, it is, as we have observed, so loosely constructed as to readily lend itself to the episodic structure Mathews finds congenial because of the wide scope of incident it allows him. It seems, then, as is often the case in Mathews' work, that the plot, used as a vehicle for description and observations of the American scene, serves Mathews well in his role of social commentator.

III   *Heroes and Fops*

The conflict between the traditional American values and those of the many mid-nineteenth-century Americans who care only for wealth, material comfort, and social status is again evident in Mathews' Thanksgiving story, *Chanticleer,* in which Sylvester Peabody, the family patriarch and veteran of the Revolution, serves a similar function to that of Job in *Moneypenny*. Like Job, old Sylvester is the embodiment of all the best American virtues: honesty, love of country, humility, and a democratic spirit. When he speaks of the days of the Revolution and the heroic past and when he envisions a glorious national future, Sylvester is a communal spokesman articulating the highest ideals of the national ethic.

In direct contrast to Sylvester are several members of the family who are motivated less by heroic ideals than by consideration of material gains or social position. His son William, the prototype of the American "self-made man," has forgotten his origins; and, finding satisfaction only in the race for the dollar, he cares little for the struggles of others. A successful landlord in New York City, he proudly announces that he has just added three new houses to his property. However, when Sylvester asks how the little holdings of his widowed daughter, Margaret, are doing, William, who manages his sister's financial affairs, replies that "rents come slowly." Sylvester laments, "in a word, the old story, the widow gets nothing again from the city. I had hopes you would be able to bring her some returns this time, for she needs it sadly."[3] Margaret's son, Elbridge, has vanished, many think to evade a murder charge; and she has, therefore, no means of support except for what Sylvester can give her. William answers, "I do the best I can, but money's not to be got out of stone walls," and then he is taken aback by Sylvester's quiet question, "my son, do you never think of that other house reserved for us all?" (25). William, who has forgotten who he is, is being called to a consideration of his background and the rigorous morality in which he was brought up. The contrast between the modest, deeply religious farmer and his son, the crass, gloating, big-city businessman, provides a good deal of insight into the course Mathews' America is pursuing.

When Sylvester and William, the father and the son, sit quietly looking over the family homeland, Sylvester thinks of the past, of friends who died freeing the country, of the Indian long gone from the landscape, of how "the darkness of the woods had retired before the cheering sun of peace and plenty"; and of how "from a little people, his dear country, for whose welfare his sword had been stained, had grown into a great nation" (27). He thinks, too, of the lost Elbridge and mourns for his family honor, stained by his grandson's guilt. On the other hand, William smugly reflects about his rise to material success:

[The scene] brought chiefly a recollection how in his early manhood he had set out from those quiet fields for a hard struggle with the world, with a bare dollar in his pocket . . . and how he had gone on step by step, forgetting all the pleasant ties of his youth, all recollections of nature and cheerful faces of friends and kinsfolk, adding thousand to thousand, house to house; building, unlike Jacob, a ladder, that descended to the lower world, up which all harsh and dark spirits perpetually thronged and joined to bring him down; and yet he smiled grimly at the thought of the power he possessed, and how many of his early acquaintances trembled before him because he was grown to be a rich man. (26)

William spends most of the Thanksgiving holiday grimly poring over old deeds, trying to increase the familial estate, thinking all the while little about family or country.

In William's younger brother, Oliver, we see an American of markedly different values and demeanor. Oliver has settled in the West and, as a result, has acquired some of the boisterousness of that region in both costume and manners. He wears his hair "at length and unshorn," his coat has "a row of great horn-buttons on either breast," and on his hands he has "enormous woolen mittens." Although he does not speak of "half-horses and half-alligators, nor of greased lightning," he does complain "most bitterly of the uncommon smoothness of the roads in these parts, the short grass, and the 'bominable want of elbow-room all over the neighborhood" (33). Perhaps Oliver's most flamboyant attribute is his great cotton pocket-handkerchief, on which is "displayed in glowing colors, by some cunning artist, the imposing scene of the signers of the Declaration of Independence getting ready to affix their names." As Mathews remarks, "Mr. Oliver Peabody [is] the politician of the family, and always had the immortal Declaration of Independence at his tongue's end or in hand" (41).

Unfortunately, the would-be politician's love of country is too often expressed in merely political terms in which a mature awareness of the American tradition and a selfless dedication to solving national problems are ignored in favor of the politician's penchant for being well liked. Therefore, although a more genial, sympathetic character than his brother William, Oliver, like his brother, lacks insight into the real values of the national way of life. Consequently, when Sylvester offers an example of American selflessness and generosity, both brothers miss the point. Sylvester tells how the late Reverend Mr. Barbary spent the time "he did not employ in prayers, preaching and tending the sick, in working the farms about, for he had no wages for preaching." When he was not working, he took a basket and "sallying through the fields, gathered berries, which he bestowed on the needy families of the neighborhood." In winter he "collected branches in the woods about as firewood for the poor." Both brothers fail to understand the moral involved in this account. Oliver, the politician, responds, "that was a capital idea, it must have made him very popular." William, the merchant, asks, "wasn't he always thought to be a little out of his head? He might have sold all the wood for a good price in severe winters" (45–46).

Perhaps even more distasteful to Mathews than the younger Peabodys' lack of understanding of the American tradition are the foreign manners affected by Sylvester's grandson, Tiffany Carrack, who is a satiric sketch of the American who has no pride in his country. He and his parvenu mother are, like the Joneses in *Moneypenny,* a mass of affectations. They value a rich façade more than they do real virtue; and, as a result, Tiffany's appearance at the Peabody homestead makes a sharp contrast with the other members of the family:

> Mr. Tiffany Carrack, with patent shanks to his boots which sprang him into the air when he walked, corsets to brace his body in, new-fangled straps to keep him down, a patent collar of peculiar invention, to hold his head aloft, moving as it were under the convoy of a company of invisible influences, deriving all his motions from the shoemaker, stay-maker, tailor, and linen-draper, who originally wound him up and set him a-going, . . . having withal, by way of paint to his ashy countenance, a couple of little conch-shell tufts, tawny yellow (that being the latest to be had at the perfumer's) on his upper lip: the representative of all the latest . . . patents and contrivances in apparel, . . . followed his excellent mother. (64)

Extremely proud of his appearance, Tiffany is not above making invidious comparisons between it and Sylvester's old, homely clothes.

Tiffany's arrival at the farm is a surprise, for the report was that he was in the West prospecting for gold. However, he got no farther than New Orleans, for there he heard that the California "natives had rebelled and wouldn't work anymore," thereby necessitating that, as Tiffany says, "if I would get any of the precious, I must dig with a shovel with my own dear digits; of course, I turned back in disgust" (65). He also reveals that he turned back in disgust from his cousin Elbridge, whom he saw in New Orleans;

for Elbridge was in tattered clothes, and Tiffany did not want to be seen with such a ragamuffin.

Obviously, Tiffany represents a departure from the pioneer tradition in America; instead of exhibiting American energy, he apes European decrepitude. He has adopted a "tottering and uncertain step, indicating a dilapidated old age, only kept together by the clothes he wears" (67). Seeing this gait, which mystifies the rest of the family, his mother remarks with an affectionate smile of maternal pride, "you remind me more and more every day, Tiff, of that dear delightful old Baden-Baden." Tiffany proudly tells the Peabodys that Baden-Baden is "only a prince of my acquaintance on the other side of the water, and a devilish clever fellow. But he couldn't stand it here, I'm afraid—everything's so new." Sylvester smilingly replies, "I'm rather old," but Tiffany says, "that ain't the thing I want exactly; I want an old castle or two and a donjon keep, and that sort of thing. You understand." Sylvester's suggestion of the old revolutionary bastion, Fort Hill, similarly leaves Tiffany cold. He gracefully articulates his meaning: "'No—no—you don't take exactly. I mean something more in the antique—something or other, you see'—here he began twirling his forefinger in the air and sketching an amorphous phantom of some sort, of an altogether unattainable character, 'in a word—Jehosaphat'" (68). This last word is a favorite of Tiffany's; having heard some blades use it, he thinks it fashionable and says it constantly.

This pseudo-European fop fancies himself a ladies' man and endeavors to woo his cousin Miriam, a sensible girl who abhors him. Unfortunately, he takes the ill-advised course of attempting to win her through the typically European manner of serenading her under the window. Attired in yellow slippers, a red silk cloak trimmed with gold, a fez cap, and white muslin turban, he places himself in the garden and begins warbling "Dearest, awake—you need not fear,/For he—for he your Troubador is here!" (73). He has inadvertently stationed himself, however, under the wrong window; and his song is floating up to the old servant woman, Mopsey, who believes that neighborhood rogues are attempting to raid the Peabody garden. Seeing Mopsey look out, the romantic Tiffany gets the wrong impression: "A gentle conviction was dawning in the brain of Mr. Carrack that this was the fair Miriam happily responding to his challenge in the appropriate character and costume of a

Moorish Princess; when, as he began to roar again, still more violent and furious in his chanting, the black head opened and demanded, 'What you want dere?' followed by an extraordinary shower of gourd-shells . . . crashing upon his sconce . . ." (74).

Juxtaposed immediately against this comic scene of ludicrous affectation receiving just retribution is Mathews' account of the Thanksgiving sermon given at the simple country church which the Peabodys attend. Here, in place of avarice, of eagerness for popular acclaim, and of vain pomp and fashion, we hear the timeless virtues of American life expounded, as the minister declares of his neighbor, "he is my brother, we are in league together, we must stand and fall by one another. Is his labor harder than mine? Surely I will ease him. Hath he no bed to be on? I have two—I will lend him one" (83). Finally, he reminds them that, as Americans, they have much for which they ought to be thankful.

Inspired by this sermon, the Peabodys return home for the holiday dinner. Sylvester, assuming his role as patriarch, speaks of family and country, and he likens the nation to a "glorious family of friendly states" (99). The Peabody dinner, with its representatives from each part of the country, tends to symbolize the national union of states indulging in a ritualistic celebration of their fraternity. The union is made complete by the sudden return of Elbridge, who has been exonerated of his supposed crime; and, in the larger, symbolic, context, this return seems to signify that all national problems and variations from the norm are merely misunderstandings and with good, democratic faith can be resolved.

Despite excessive sentimentality and a tedious story line, *Chanticleer* is not the "rankest imaginable effort to do for the American Thanksgiving what Dickens did for Christmas" that Perry Miller calls it.[4] Again using the plot merely as a vehicle for observation of the American scene, Mathews pictures life in rural America, still close to the customs and values that led, in part, to the founding of the nation; and he contrasts this way of life with the degenerate forms of behavior to which it has given birth. Mathews here is dealing with a subject of gigantic proportions, working with the materials of tragedy on a national scale. Although he does not have the talent to put them all together into a work commensurate with his subject, he is perceptive enough to sense the direction in which the country is going and to provide at least a sketch of the situation.

IV   False Pretences

The European-inspired foppery and ostentation of Tiffany Carrack in *Chanticleer* are part of a general foolishness which Mathews
sees taking hold of the more affluent segments of American society;
it makes otherwise sensible people deprecate their own nation and
affect European manners in an ill-advised effort to aggrandize their
social standing. This situation receives its fullest examination in
Mathews' comedy of manners *False Pretences* (1856), a play in
which he again contrasts traditional American virtues, as manifested
in rural life and characters with the shallow ideals and foreign-
inspired fopperies of modern urban society. The earliest example
of this kind of American play is Royall Tyler's *The Contrast,* but
Mathews seems to have been most strongly influenced by Anna
Cora Mowatt's *Fashion* (1845), a play which treats the same subject as *False Pretences* but which, to a great extent, avoids the gross
caricatures which Mathews presents in this generally unsuccessful
work.

As is usually the case in Mathews' work, the plot is a patchwork
affair. Frank Whittemore, a struggling young lawyer, has brought
suit against the Milledollar family, claiming that the will of his
grandfather Peter Pandelly, through which the Milledollars gained
their wealth, was, in fact, superseded by a later will leaving the
entire inheritance to him. He offers a generous settlement out of
court, but the Milledollars scornfully reject his offer. Finally, with
the aid of the beautiful Widow Golden and that of the poor but
kind Crockerys, who are disavowed relatives of the newly rich
Milledollars, Whittemore wins his case, marries the Widow Golden,
and reunites the Crockerys and the Milledollars.

More important than the plot is the contrast Mathews builds
between his primary target, the Milledollars and their coterie—a
group of rank parvenus whose money gives them delusions of
grandeur making them forget they are of the same common American stock as their fellows—and the Crockerys, a family of good
sense and democratic spirit who represent the best of the continuing
American tradition. The Milledollars have cut them from their list
of acquaintances because of Adam Crockery's business failure,
brought about by ill-advised charity to an old friend. It appears
that when the Milledollars cut the Crockerys, they are symbolically

cutting themselves off from such traditional American virtues as kindliness and generosity.

Mathews takes us into the Crockery home in order that we may observe the way of life against which that of the Milledollars is measured and found wanting. The stage directions pointedly describe the Crockery living room as *"plainly furnished,"* thus emphasizing the lack of ostentation and affectation in the family's tastes. Instead, we find the homely good cheer and unassuming virtues which have made America great. We observe Adam Crockery relating a long-standing joke to his family—although they have all heard it many times before, it never fails to please them:

Mrs. Crockery. I can never hear, that story, Adam, of young Clem and the meal-bag without a good laugh.

Eva. And, Pa, did he really put the stone in one end and the grain in the other, to balance it on Old Sorrel's back?[5]

Adam laughingly replies that it is just as he told her so often before, and they all laugh again. Thus, we see that, although they live in the city, the Crockerys, unlike the Milledollars, keep alive their ties with their rural background and thereby maintain qualities of freshness and purity not found in New York high society. Crockery is named "Adam" with good reason, as Mathews indulges in his American primitivism.

Unlike most of those in New York, the Crockerys are content with their lot. Not being status-seekers, they do not repine over their loss of social position; for their values are more lasting than those of any self-consciously "fashionable" society. Consequently, Mrs. Crockery can ingenuously remark to her husband and daughter, "you may miss your handsome books of the new library, with plates and gilt edges, and their fine reading, but here's a Book worth all the libraries in the world put together." Crockery agrees, "the old Family Bible. You never spoke more like an inspired person, yourself, Margaret" (24). Mawkish as these statements sound, to these people such words are not mere ostentatiously pious cant; they are a code to live by, and Crockery lives by them to the extent of ruining himself financially through his charity.

In the Crockery house, a pair of doors, hidden by a drapery, connects their home with that of the Milledollars. This improbable situation is a result of a clause in Peter Pandelly's will which demanded that the heir reside in the old Pandelly home or face forfeiture of the legacy. Milledollar, the heir, refused to live in such a humble dwelling; but, seeing the need, nevertheless, to comply with the wording of the will, if not its spirit, he built a more magnificent house for his own dwelling and attached it to the old Pandelly home, which he never enters. Less pretentious, the Crockerys were pleased to move into their late relation's home, and, therefore, live next door to their more stylish relations, who, not happy with the situation, keep the connecting doors locked and draped. To Mathews, the connecting households, actually part of one large building, are a representation of the national condition. The United States, in other words, houses both traditional virtue and honesty and a more modern materialism and foppery.

The differences between the Crockerys and the Milledollars are evident the first time we see them together as they discuss the prospective suitors for Milledollar's daughter. Asked his opinion, Crockery declares in favor of Whittemore, "if you mean to consult your daughter's happiness, you will prefer the poor lawyer, who is honest and kind." However, Milledollar and his hedonistic friend, Doctor Cram, opt for Peter Funk, who, although neither honest nor kind, is "a speculator of rising merit," and, as Doctor Cram says, has a "keener eye for business than ever sharpened the head" of any mortal he has ever met (10).

This contrast between Crockery's method of rating a man's worth by his character, and the Milledollar method of evaluating him by calculating his wealth and social status, is accentuated by the entrance into the Milledollar home of a visitor from France, Monsieur Boquet, a barber looking for work. Seeing the phrase *Son Empereur,* in Boquet's letter of introduction, Milledollar and Doctor Cram, not knowing French, mistakenly believe that Boquet is the Emperor's son and not, as the letter states, his barber. This error leads Milledollar and Cram to humble themselves before this barber and to invite him as an honored guest into the Milledollar home, where he receives unlimited adulation. On the other hand, the level-headed Crockery says to Cram, "By the way, Doctor, the Emperor has no grown-up sons." To which Cram replies, "you forget—not by the *present* wife." Crockery can only add, sarcastically, "Oh, I understand. It's all the same, he has the royal blood" (12–13).

Boquet's entrance into their home comes at a propitious time for the Milledollars, for they are in the midst of their struggle for social position, and such a "find" as a distinguished foreigner like Boquet will go a long way toward bringing them into a fashionable social sphere. Their single-minded and usually clumsy drive for status often makes the Milledollars seem both comic and pathetic, as in the scene in which the Milledollars ask their daughter to show off her French for Monsieur Boquet, by translating his letter:

Milledollar. Well, Flory, you are a good French scholar; you had two quarters' French at Madame Parleyvou's school (and she charged like thunder, too!). Come, Flory, do you read it for your Ma.

Miss Milledollar. *(perusing letter)* I can't make much of these words—the French handwriting is so hard to make out! Ah, here it is—Charming, *Empereur,* and *il voyage comme vous mane!*—Why, Pa, Mons. Boquet has come to stay with us *beaucoup*—for a long time! Isn't that delightful?

Mrs. Milledollar. The regular nobility style! We shall entertain you to the best of our humble abilities. We shall provide the best the market affords, while you honor us with your patronage, and hope to give entire satisfaction by our promptitude and despatch. (15–16)

Boquet answers in his broken English with an unintentionally apt malapropism, "Madame, you are very good and extremement much ridicule" (16). As if to back up his wife's words, Milledollar has already presented Boquet with his best 1811 Madeira, only to have the Frenchman immediately judge it as "slops," leading the swindled Milledollar to lament his gullibility, "that rascally importer has imposed on me! I paid $5 a bottle for that wine, Monsieur" (13). Unfortunately, chagrin over the wine does not prevent Milledollar from bragging about his other expensive possessions. With the consummate lack of taste and grace which all too often characterizes the *nouveau riche,* Milledollar can proudly declare of his paintings, "there's one picture is nine feet long, and five broad, and it cost me seventy-five dollars" (19). The only member of the Milledollar family who is aware of its foolishness is Balaam, the unhappy son, who can do nothing but lament repeatedly, "they never understand me."

But not only the Milledollars are foolish and corrupt, for Mathews shows us that their whole circle of friends is rife with evil and stupidity. In Peter Funk, the rising young speculator, Yankee in-

genuity is perverted by greed and low cunning. Funk is introduced
by Milledollar to Monsieur Boquet as a "first-rate specimen of our
[American] kind of smartness, a successful businessman who never
puts his hand to anything that he don't make money out of it, and
somebody else don't lose by" (16). Funk has discovered the first
"placer" in California; built the finest Clipper ship in the world, on
a model of his own; and raised the tallest Gas Chimney in the world,
again on a model of his own contrivance. From these exploits he
has made a fortune which has only prompted him to want another,
larger, one. Boquet, impressed by all these accomplishments, asks
whether the gold mine and the inventions are still in operation.
Funk replies, "not one of them! The California placer turned out to
be a quartz rock, the ship wouldn't sail, the chimney wouldn't draw."
Surprisingly, Funk seems to be more pleased with the shady manner
in which he made his fortune than he would be had his projects
been honest and successful: "I sold out the placer before it was
found out, for $25,000, the Government took the Clipper off my
hands (to encourage democratic inventions) at a premium of
$10,000, and the people, scared to death with an idea that the chim-
ney would fall, moved out of the neighborhood, the land fell in
value—bought it all up for a song,—took down the chimney, and
sold out in three months, with a clear profit of about $100,000.
Rather smart wasn't it? I reckon you haven't been in this country
long" (17).

Like many American businessmen of his era, Funk works to make
money for no other reason than its attainment. He mentions in a
soliloquy that since he was only seven years old the words, "Peter
Funk, you must be a millionaire," have been ringing in his ears. He
murmurs, "there goes Peter Funk, the millionaire! Ain't that
musical!" (18). However, he associates nothing with being a millionaire, other than the title. He has no plans, no ideals, nothing which
can give his life meaning either for others or for himself. In Funk
and Milledollar, Mathews shows us two aspects of the American
self-made success, a type that is only happy in the act of making
money. Once he has it, he does not know what to do with it; and
he either wastes it extravagantly like Milledollar in an ill-conceived
attempt to gain some fuzzily defined social position or, like Funk,
exists as nothing but the personification of a growing bank account.
Better by far, as Mathews wants us to see, is to be like the unassum-

ing, contented Adam Crockerys and the Sylvester Peabodys of the nation.

In a society in which inventors do not invent but only defraud, it is not surprising that we should see professional men who do not conscientiously practice their profession. Thus, Doctor Cram is more concerned with leading the good life than with healing the sick; indeed, it seems that he views the Hippocratic oath merely as a vow delivering himself to hedonism. Mathews presents Cram involved in a tortuous decision-making process in an unusually difficult case:

> On my soul, this is truly a hard and trying case! I have practised medicine in this city, twenty years, and have never encountered anything that so moved my bowels! A fine, fat turtle at Mr. Partland's—dejeurner a la fourchette, at twelve. Early salmon [looking at notes] at Seyder's. Monthly Hardware Dinner, to his out of town customers, at five. Potomac ducks at young Maltdrop's Birthday Supper, at nine, P.M. All today. [in great distress] Oh, Lord, what shall I do? Three or four critical patients that must be looked after this day! Now if I had a friend or two to stand by me in this extremity I might work my way out. (33–34)

Cram finds a friend, Mr. Berryman, willing to stand by him for a slight remuneration, and he hurriedly gives him a summary of treatment for each patient, then runs off contentedly for a day of pleasant dining. Unfortunately, though, it seems that Cram's patients will have a less pleasant time of it; for Cram's courier has hopelessly muddled the directions given him and cannot distinguish the prescriptions from the sumptuous bill of fare which Cram has described.

In this New York society, as Mathews describes it, it is apparent that little matters except wealth, comfort, and social standing. Self-respect and dignity count for little. Consequently, even getting kicked is a means of rising in social esteem. When Berryman, serving as an emissary for Funk, duns the Crockerys for a note outstanding to the "rising speculator," he is paid and ordered from the premises by Whittemore, who threatens to kick him if he does not leave immediately. Berryman regrets that he did not avail himself of the opportunity of being kicked:

> I wish he had done it. A good kicking would give my popularity a hoist upwards. What a sensation it would create in the upper circles. Berryman kicked! Kicked! The important Berryman—the Sexton at the fashionable

church—the manager of all fashionable parties—the darling of the old women, and the chaperone of the young men! Look at the sympathy, at the condolements, at the presents! (36)

He tells Dr. Cram that the only reason he did not let Whittemore kick him was that he did not wish to be kicked in a private home: "I'll be kicked in a public square where everybody can see it. . . . It shall be done in the blaze of day" (36). Funk, discussing the threat, wishes that it had been made to him; for, had he been kicked, he could have made a good deal of money in a lawsuit.

With no self-dignity, with no meaningful sense of values, this society not surprisingly humbles itself before foreigners, obsequiously imitating their manners and flocking to their lectures. Balaam Milledollar, obviously speaking for Mathews, decries the national disgrace, a situation in which Americans, despite being "among the most knowing people of the earth" and equal to all the practical demands of a great destiny, "tend to fall prey, like children or simpletons, to any pretender who has been dipped in the salt water of the Atlantic Ocean! Does anybody understand me?" (33). As if bearing out Balaam's statement, Berryman arranges a public lecture for Boquet, who will speak on perfumes; and he has no doubt that the lecture will be well attended, for Boquet *is* a Frenchman. However, he realizes that the competition is stiff, for also in town are such foreign attractions as the "celebrated danseuse" Signora Oiliani, who stands on one toe fifteen minutes, and the "illustrious" Signor Desperado, "the great Italian Profundo Basso, whose voice comes out of his boots and rolls out of his mouth like a fireball, and explodes and rises, and falls, and diverges" (51).

The only native entertainment which seemingly finds favor with fashionable Americans is that which gives an opportunity to display their newly gained wealth. One of the most enjoyable events of recent memory was the funeral of one old Moneybags, a millionaire. Berryman calls the whole affair "as merry as a first-rate comedy," for "money's the way here; and as there had been a private reading of his will, everybody knew just how matters stood." There was a "fine legacy for the parson, who could scarcely keep a straight mouth to read the burial service" and the "whole line of mourning coaches lighted up with happy faces as [they] went down Diamond Avenue" (51–52).

Although the Milledollars know it is difficult to match such festive occasions as that of Moneybags' funeral, they attempt to impress society with a gala costume ball, which Mathews uses to supply his resolution and denouement in *False Pretences*. At this absurdly extravagant party, the Milledollars are aptly dressed: the misunderstood Balaam is a sphinx, the clothes and jewel-loving Miss Milledollar is dressed as the scandalous Madame de Pompadour, Milledollar is Napoleon, and his wife is dressed as the market woman she was when Milledollar married her. She is not sure she likes this costume, but the Widow Golden told her it would be most fetching. During the party a band of wild-looking men in rough clothes, long hair, and beards rush in. Returned prospectors from California, they have come to New York for a raucous celebration; and Berryman, who has been commissioned by the Milledollars to swell the ranks at their ball by inviting contingents from fashionable hotels around the city, has inadvertently invited this crew. Of course, too rugged and "American" to be accepted at such an effete gathering, they are sent packing. This interruption is followed by a more devastating one, for word comes that the Supreme Court has awarded Pandelly's legacy to Whittemore. When he takes possession of Milledollar's house and throws open the doors connecting it with the adjoining house, he reveals the Crockerys still sitting contentedly and laughing over the story of Young Clem and his trip to the mill. Thus, we see, ultimately, the triumph of American decency and good sense over villainy, pretense, and stupidity.

As may be obvious from this discussion, *False Pretences* is a weakly constructed burlesque. Its characters are often grotesque caricatures drawn from the better characterizations in Tyler's *The Contrast* and Miss Mowatt's *Fashion;* thus, we see clumsily depicted the unduly fashion-conscious parvenus, the idolized foreigners, and Americans who retain their traditional good sense. Peter Funk, however, is an interesting creation who serves as an early example of the robber barons who were to amass great fortunes in an often brutal manner in the latter part of the nineteenth century.

Weak as *False Pretences* may be, it cannot be ignored, for it is part of Mathews' overriding appraisal of his contemporary American society. The foibles and social failings it portrays, however awkwardly, are part of the national way of life and must be faced and overcome. Americans must live with the sense of honor and tradition that Sylvester Peabody, Job Moneypenny, and Adam Crockery evince or, as Mathews shows, the whole nation will be one large society for the advancement of imposture.

Although the view of American values and manners that Mathews gives us in these works is, generally, a rather superficial one, it is so almost of necessity; for he endeavors to treat Americans in their role as social animals, by describing the way they appear to each other and to themselves and by depicting their foolish ploys as they attempt to fool others but end, instead, as only their own dupes. The value of this effort resides in Mathews' ability to hold up to America a slightly distorted mirror which caricatures the foibles of the nation, casting them back as a series of colorful, amusing incidents with pointed morals.

CHAPTER 6

The American Political Scene

I *In Defense of the American Political System*

A major aspect of Mathews' description of the American scene involves his efforts to bring his countrymen to an awareness of the political responsibilities their citizenship entails. In his political writings, including plays, fiction, poems, and essays, he deplores the excesses of factionalism, demagoguery, and corruption into which the American political system often slips; and he advocates, in their stead, adherence to principles of honesty, selflessness, and high-minded statesmanship. This does not mean that Mathews, a democrat, inspired by the ideals of Jackson, lost faith in the American political system; rather, he cared enough about it to want it purged of its shortcomings. His comedy, *The Politicians* (1840), and his novel of city life, *The Career of Puffer Hopkins* (1842), satirize the political scene in general, and many of the sketches in *Yankee Doodle* (1846–47), Mathews' magazine of topical humor, sarcastically comment on specific governmental actions of the period in particular. Based on his firsthand observations of American election campaigns and office holders, Mathews formulated several theories about national politics; these receive their most explicit statement in several articles he wrote for *Arcturus,* the magazine he co-edited with Evert Duyckinck in 1841 and 1842.

The political situation in the New York of which Mathews writes was an ugly one, and, as Gustavus Myers points out in his *The History of Tammany Hall,* the influence of New York politics and campaign tactics was a strong one throughout the nation, for what worked there was tried elsewhere; thus, when Mathews speaks of the political scene in New York, he speaks, in effect, of the American scene at large. Myers describes the depravity of New York government in Mathews' era as pervasive, as not restricted to merely that one favorite whipping boy of reformers, Tammany Hall: "The Whigs, for instance, sought in every possible way to outdo Tammany in election frauds; they stuffed ballot boxes, colonized voters, employed rowdies and thugs at the polls and distributed thousands of deceptive ballots for the use of their opponents. In fiscal frauds, likewise, they left a record well-nigh equaling that of Tammany. The Native Americans imitated both Whigs and Tammany men, and the Republicans [gave] instances at Albany of a wholesale venality unapproached in the history of legislative bodies."[1]

Myers describes in more detail the underhanded methods used by the politicans of Mathews' contemporary America: the rabble-rousing harangues which frequently fomented riots in the city streets, the ballot-box stuffing, the vote-buying, the intimidation of voters which often made elections a fraud, and the corruption and influence peddling of all too many office holders (94–149). One of the more outrageous ploys in picking up extra votes was that of allowing convicts to escape from the prison on Blackwell's Island on condition that they vote as their keepers ordered them. Similarly, almshouse paupers were used as illicit voters.

II *Satirizing the Machine*

This dishonesty in campaign and government Mathews satirizes in *The Politicians,* and he attacks the same political failings which H. H. Brackenridge had used as his targets forty years earlier in *Modern Chivalry.* The men whom Mathews describes as seeking office are no more suited for it than were Teague O'Regan and most of the other aspiring politicians in Brackenridge's novel, and the demagogic appeals to the crowd in each case are similar. Cooper, too, through his Aristabulus Bragg in *Home as Found,* attacked a situation in which many of the least likely men in the community were candidates for public office. However, in *The Politicans,* which is exclusively a depiction of several aspects of the American political system, Mathews provides more extensive portrayal of its short-comings than did either Brackenridge or Cooper.

Throughout *The Politicians* we see office seekers who willingly sacrifice morality and a sense of decency in order to enhance their chances of election. Mr. Brisk, candidate for alderman, plans to gain a few votes by using the church bells. This perversion of religious practice is an excellent device, for "many of the more quiet voters, being accustomed to its Sunday summons, would be brought out and would readily aid our ticket, if they understood the steeple, for the time, to be in the hands of our party." Furthermore, the sexton might be employed to read prayers for their side from a small window in the steeple.[2] Getting word of Brisk's plans, his opponent, Gudgeon, tries to win back the religious vote by having one of his henchmen climb to the top of the steeple and deliver a harangue: "it might do away with the evil influence of the proceedings below, and give us a tremendous ascendancy at once" (123).

As might be expected in a campaign involving such degrading tactics, the candidates do not intelligently debate issues, for issues do not matter. Of real importance, though, are the candidates' relative abilities to affect shabby clothing, their talents at moving a mob with soaring bombast and inflated rhetoric, and the efficacy of the deceitful practices of each in padding his own vote and in keeping that of his opponents down. Therefore, ingenious devices must be thought up to show a candidate off to his best advantage. One such plan is to have Gudgeon walk down a crowded street with a drunkard on each arm, an action which his campaign manager assures him will sweep all segments of the electorate to his cause. First, and perhaps most importantly, it is an attention-getting device; and, as we know full well at mid-twentieth century, any candidate needs "exposure." Moreover, Gudgeon's walk is calculated to aid his "image" immensely; "Gudgeon is friendly to tavern licence—we'll vote for him," the tavern keepers will say, "obvious from his respect for our customers." However, the temperance vote need not be alienated; for, if Gudgeon puts his mouth "cunningly" to the ear of his companions and lifts up his fingers in a solemn manner, it will look as if he is "warning the poor wretches to refrain from their cups." At the same time, the "common mob" (a sizable voting bloc) will laugh, "taking the whole spectacle for a very tolerable joke." Gudgeon believes he can aid the effect by having some tracts against drunkenness sticking from his coat pockets, while, at the same time, some large handbills, declaring that he is in favor of retail liquor shops, might be posted up on the opposite fence (123–24).

Mathews also satirizes political oratory when, to keep his campaign going at a high pitch, Gudgeon asks his lieutenant, Glib, to exert himself at public meetings: "ride high, sir—ride high. Express your willingness to die for your country—in the last—in the deepest, ditch" (131). The lieutenant needs little encouragement, for he is always ready to send the patriotic rhetoric soaring:

Glib. Sons of men that dared/To blow a blast of stern defiance/On the trump—
Citizen (*to his neighbor*). Now we'll have something nice; he's always good on trumpets.
Glib. Of patriotic fire that shook/These soup-fed tyrants in the chairs of power: —/ That you it was, who raised the bloody flag—
Citizen. His flags, if such a thing be possible, is better than his trumpets. (140)

Attention-getting devices, wild promises, and patriotic declamations are not considered sufficient, however, to ensure a candidate's election; efforts even more blatant than these must be carried out if an office seeker is to gain victory. Therefore, Brisk hires foul-smelling bums to set up a stench at polling places in Gudgeon wards in an effort to keep the opposition voters away; and he also uses hoodlums to beat up those Gudgeon supporters who have the courage to make their way past the odoriferous bums.

The cynicism of New York politicians is pointed up by Mathews when he informs his audience that not only is the campaign aimed at deluding and coercing the voters; it is, without their knowledge, also financed by them. The parties use tax money in order to pay their campaign expenses and, even worse, the costs of their rather lavish entertainments. Brisk's manager suggests "for the sake of appearances" that they can diminish their committee expenses a bit; "we can smoke half a box [of cigars] and carry none away; we can leave the candle-ends for next evening, and not throw them at any clean person we may see passing through the street; a quart of beer a-piece should satisfy us" (133).

Mathews also shows that, in spite of their appeals to the common man in a blatant effort at courting his vote, the politicians care little for him; indeed, they often dismiss him and his needs with abhorrence. Brisk, avowedly the poor man's candidate, is outraged when his daughter falls in love with the penniless young musician Blanding. When it is suggested to Brisk that Blanding may be his equal, he angrily retorts, "my equal! Sir, he is a paltry flute-player at the theater—a twelve shilling a-week whistler and inspirer of dead wood" (127). This contempt for one's constituents is, as Mathews indicates, not peculiar to candidate-for-alderman Brisk; it seems to reach even to national figures in Washington. When Blanding plans to disguise himself as the relative of a United States senator, he is told that he must acquire the manners and opinions of those in power in the capital—he must "speak contemptuously of American habits, intellect, society, commerce, literature, and American things generally" (142).

It seems, however, that the politician's lack of regard for his constituents is balanced by his adoration and fear of those who are in positions of greater power than his own. Thus, it is not surprising that Blanding, masquerading as a Senator's grandnephew, is not only welcomed into Brisk's home but is attended with the greatest obsequiousness. Brisk is overjoyed and overawed: "I am in the same house, under the same roof with the grand-nephew of a Senator. I hear the creaking of his boots! Hark—he coughed! He is on the stairs. Was I entitled to expect this? What weight and character this will give to my canvass, that I have been closeted with a functionary's near relative" (135). Needless to say, Brisk believes the Senator's grandnephew would make a perfect match for his daughter.

Sneering at the public and caring little for its well-being, the politician still seeks office; the reasons, Mathews shows us, for this apparent contradiction are compelling and obvious—power and graft. Gudgeon, in a soliloquy, speaks of his pleasure in seeing his name broadcast over the district: "every spile becomes a speaker of [my] praises . . . and there's not a dead wall that does not announce [my] glory in the largest capitals" (122). In his pride, Gudgeon has forgotten his humble, rural background and the common people of whom he was a part. Similarly, Brisk has forgotten the people and greedily anticipates with his henchman the fruits of office: "If we succeed, as we must—look at the prospect, it's almost enough to bring tears into one's eyes—you shall be made a contractor for the almshouse, and have a nice little profit on every morsel that goes into a pauper's mouth: a perfect prince of a contractor: and not a candle shall be sniffed in the establishment,—nor an eyelid dropped, without you having clipped the tallow and discounted the drug for both" (139). Brisk, moreover, has plans for himself, and one of his first acts upon entering office will be to have a certain lane broadened into an avenue which will take away the short front lots of the other citizens along the route but bring some of his land to the street, thereby increasing its value. He smugly declares that "all this shall be done for the good of the people, the health of the neighborhood, or any other patriotic and high-minded considerations" (140).

The candidates' lack of faith in the common man turns out to be unjustified in this election, however; for old Zachary Crumb, a friend of Blanding's and a simple, honest patriot, is urged to run for office and is elected in a landslide by a people who are tired of campaign hokum and of the corruption of men in power. Crumb's election represents the triumph of the true American tradition of virtue and love of country. One old citizen declares, "I have seen old men like myself here today that have not cast a ballot before for the last fifteen years" and have come out to vote for Crumb; "I have seen such men, that apparently tarried in the world but to deposit a vote for Crumb" (141). Youth, too, has rallied to support the old man, sensing that he offers it something valuable, a sense of sharing in an American tradition, which the modern political hacks do not even know exists. Mathews invests Crumb's cause and victory with religious overtones when he writes of supernatural signs giving portents of the old patriot's election. One citizen asks, "did you mark when the sky was overcast this morning, how the sun shone on Crumb's name on the banner, while the rest was in darkness?" (141). Another declares that "they say when Brisk entered to give his own vote, the eagle that his friends had perched on a staff above the door, shrieked and dropped his wings" (141). Mathews' use of such omens shows that he equates the sanctity of the American tradition with that of religion, and he sees them both protected under God's aegis.

In *The Politicians,* then, we see Mathews' satirical depiction of the American political system, which he conceives to have gone wrong and become mired in lies and corruption; but also we see his faith in the common man's ability to see through lies, ultimately, and to work to reaffirm the values of the republic by supporting public servants who care about the people's needs.

III   *The Making of a Politician*

The Career of Puffer Hopkins also satirizes the political scene in America, in this case through Mathews' depiction of the initiation of Puffer Hopkins, an idealistic young man from the country, into the workings of a big-city political machine. That the young man emerges relatively unscathed indicates once more that Mathews does not believe that the evil which has tainted American life is unsurmountable.

Puffer is first seen as he attends a political rally, immediately upon his arrival in New York from the country. The rally, held, aptly enough, in a "large, misshapen building,"[3] is a tedious affair; it is replete with drinking, shouting, and rabble-rousing demagoguery, all to little purpose. At a pause in the proceedings which, to the discomfiture of the crowd, no speaker can be found to fill, the young unknown, Puffer Hopkins, volunteers to speak on the issue which the audience finds most pressing, whether or not to support plans for the construction of a new aquaduct. Puffer takes the issue extremely seriously and offers an idealistic speech ingenuously invoking all the venerable principles of American democracy to which knowing politicians usually appeal as a formula of lip service. He declares, timidly, at first, that he is aware he is "rash and foolhardy . . . in coming before so intelligent an audience at that critical moment" (13). However, he declares that he is "actuated and impelled by a sense of duty," which will not allow him to keep silent "while that great question calls for an advocate." He then reasons profoundly that "taxation is not democracy" (13). His speech wins the plaudits of the audience, and he steps down from the platform, triumphant.

In the crowd at the rally is the politically knowledgeable old man Hobbleshank, who decides that young Puffer has the potential to go far in politics but needs some coaching. Introducing himself, he congratulates Puffer, but tells him he still has much to learn. Through Hobbleshank's instructions on how to deliver a political speech, Mathews adds to the satire on political oratory which he began in *The Politicans*. First, Hobbleshank says, Puffer must not take the stage again without his coat "buttoned snug to the chin, which shows that you mean to give them a resolute speech—a devilish resolute speech, . . . full of storm and thunder, sir." Second, "there was a very awful and unpardonable omission" in Puffer's talk, "where were your banners? You hadn't one in your whole speech." He wonders how Puffer could address a speech to a political assembly in New York, without "a tatter of bunting in the whole of it." He explains: "An army might as well go into battle as an orator into our popular meetings, without his flags and standards. Where were your stars, too? There wasn't even the twinkle of a comet's tail in the whole harrangue: they expect it. Stars are the pepper and salt of a political discourse—mind that if you please" (17). Hobbleshank adds that rather than address himself to a gentlemanly looking member of the audience, Puffer should use as his target "a poor scamp—the beggarliest in the house [with] an understanding like granite rock." It is this man's intelligence to which he must speak, for this is the true intellectual level of a crowd at a political gathering (18). Finally, he tells Puffer not to spare emphatic and wild gesticulating, such as at the crescendo of his speech leaping onto a chair, waving a hat, and calling upon the audience "to die for their country, their families and their firesides —or any other convenient reason" (21). This sort of excitement the crowd loves.

Puffer's efforts under the tutelage of Hobbleshank soon bring him into favor with the political powers of the district, who appoint him to the "Vigilance Committee"; this appointment enables Mathews to give his readers an inside account of the election process in New York and to use the viewpoint of Puffer, who works as a small-time political hack for the committee. One of the party bosses explains Puffer's duties to him: they entail spying on the voters and reporting on their personal habits in order that their tastes may be ascertained and the most efficacious appeals can be made to them at election time. Also, Puffer is "to go along the wharves, and up into the alleys, and down into the cellers and inquire for voters—disseminating the right doctrine by the way, and making everybody of your opinion by having no opinion at all" (58). As part of the campaign to win the hearts and minds of voters, Puffer is admonished to find out whether there are any old women on his beat "to give iron spectacles to or small children— to nurse with gingerbread," or any recent deaths "that [he] may sympathize in the bereavement, by wearing a strip of crepe on [his] hat" (58). Thus, we see that the political effort is a comprehensive and tireless one requiring an army of hacks who let little escape their ken.

As a municipal election draws near, Puffer's duties mount, and Mathews depicts the increasingly sordid tactics as the pace of political activity quickens. Hoboes and transient sailors must be taught to impersonate legal voters; convicts brought across the river from the penitentiary on Blackwell's Island must be scrubbed clean so they can be presentable at the polls when they vote the straight party ticket; and scurrilous posters must be put up defaming the honor of the candidates of the other parties. No less scurrilous speeches must be made denouncing the opposition and further inflaming the already fired-up voters who have been liberally plied with cheap rotgut liquor. Mathews describes one speaker as pacing up and down the platform, "swaying his arms and foaming at the mouth, as though he were in a cage, roaring to be let out" (179). Indeed, most of Mathews' description of the campaign, particularly as it gets closer to the hectic three days of the election itself, is delivered in terms of animal imagery, as he provides an implicit commentary on the violence and ugliness which too often distort the electoral process in America.

The chief candidates, who head their party's ticket by running for mayor, do what they can to inspire such vicious campaign tactics. They are unprincipled scoundrels, who, although purporting to represent the "people" or "property," are, in fact, concerned only with furthering their own dishonest aims. Both candidates trade on the dreams of the more unfortunate voters and try to buy them with promises that can never be kept, so that, in essence, the voters "flattered themselves that they and their families were as good as provided for" and "went in and voted for one or the other, according as they preferred the fare, lodgings and accommodation held out by either party" (187).

The political system of which such a campaign is a manifestation is one which Mathews derides continually for its inefficiency, corruption, and unshakable self-righteousness. The only sustained effort of which it is capable is for the maintenance of the existing situation. Nothing is attempted that might deal with the real problems of the great numbers of people in the country. Consequently, the villain of the novel, the miserly and lecherous old landlord, Fyler Close, who has broken up Hobbleshank's home by kidnapping his son, and thus, in effect, killing his wife, and who has ruined the lives of many people as a usurer and slumlord, is apprehended and punished only when he deliberately starts a fire that destroys the property of a powerful insurance company. It is evident that, under the existing political conditions, people are not so important as property.

In spite of Mathews' satirical attack in *Puffer Hopkins* on American political life, it seems that, as in *The Politicians,* he retains some faith in America's ability to redeem the situation and make its governmental apparatus the kind of mechanism it was meant to be. In this novel a do-nothing congressman dies, and Puffer Hopkins is elected to take his place in Washington. Although initiated into the corruption that permeates American politics, Puffer seems to have retained much of his idealism and, perhaps, will give the public the kind of support that it ought to have. On the other hand, it would be misleading to infer this as a complete vindication of the system, for the congressman's death is merely a fortuitous happening, not the sort of thing that reformers can count on. Furthermore, despite his good nature, Puffer's unthinking acceptance of political chicanery does not reveal the kind of sophistication needed to change things.

One of the charges leveled at *The Career of Puffer Hopkins* and *The Politicians* is that Mathews has crudely caricatured nature.[4] He defends himself by claiming that he is "a writer of the humorous," and, as such, caricature falls within the province of his work. He cites Cervantes, Smollett, and Fielding as authors of the kind of work he is trying to do. Like them, he tries to avoid a "servile transcript of every-day objects" and, instead, attempts to "discover in nature the germ of character, and to expand it . . . into a livelier, truer development than nature, in her ordinary moods, presents."[5] However, Mathews seems to lapse into clumsy caricature, without a living characterization in either work; and, while satire obviously is often a potent means of political commentary, it seems that, for Mathews' criticism to be effective, there must be more in the way of showing the problems of real people and what results from their confrontations with the existing political situations. While his descriptions of political phenomena such as mass meetings, torch-light processions, and congressional debates are successful, his frequent inability in these satires to present actual people and their exigencies keeps him from getting to the crux of the situation and from showing its failures where they are most damning.

IV   *Topical Commentary*

More topical and somewhat more effective is the satire in *Yankee Doodle* (October 3, 1846—October 2, 1847), the weekly humor magazine which was started largely as a result of Mathews' instigation and which he edited from July 3, 1847, until the last issue on October 2 of that year. Before he assumed control, Mathews was one of the regular contributors to the journal, which was primarily under the editorship of George Foster.[6] Unfortunately, all of the articles in *Yankee Doodle* are unsigned ones; and, though we know the authorship of a small scattering of them because of Evert Duyckinck's initialings in the first few issues and his comments in his diary and correspondence about several others, for the vast majority we cannot be certain of the authors' identities.[7]

There are, however, a number of articles which internal evidence leads me to believe were probably done by Mathews. The evidence consists of similarities between these articles and Mathews' other work in terms of subject matter (such striking local scenes as Blackwell's Island and the Bowery and such local types as the seamstress and lower-class urban tough); themes (the stupidity and corruption of all too many politicians and the misunderstanding of the relations between the American political process and the social scene); and technique (broad caricature, sentimentality for purposes of social criticism, and use of dialect). Though such subjects, themes, and techniques are not, of course, peculiar to Mathews' work, nevertheless, when several of them appear in the same article, combined often with an abrasive, frequently pontificating tone found in his writings, I strongly suspect Mathews to be the author.

The chief reason for the relative effectiveness of the satirical pieces contributed by Mathews to *Yankee Doodle* is that the satire is tied to specific events, rather than to the general abuses attacked in *The Politicians* and *Puffer Hopkins,* and this seems to exert a moderating influence on Mathews' tendency toward caricature which is often too far-fetched to be successful. Moreover, the limitations in space of the article form itself seem to help Mathews focus more effectively on a specific abuse, thus making frequently for a more incisive commentary than we find in his earlier efforts at political satire.

Yankee Doodle's general aims are set forth clearly in the lead

article of the first issue. This item, "Yankee Doodle Comes to Town"
—identified by Duyckinck's initialings as Mathews' work—speaks
of Mr. Yankee Doodle's compassion: "If Yankee Doodle sees
one down under oppression, he will raise him up: if up and hard
bestead by odds, he will spring to his side and fight for him to the
last breath." Moreover, the author enumerates the targets of his
scorn: "The object of any paper bearing my name shall be *the
propagation of true, genuine Yankee-Doodleism; and the utter
extirpation of old Fudgeism and Monkeyism in* Art, Literature,
Society, the Drama, *and all other provinces* of national labor."[8]
Mathews closes by predicting glorious success for Mr. Yankee
Doodle and the nation this heroic comic figure will serve:

> Having knocked down many a tall woodland in his day, with his axe,
> he now carries it to wield against high-headed and braggart abuses which
> spread their leaves among his people; and our private judgment is, he
> will swing it so freely and with so good effect, the day will yet come when
> there will not stand in all the breadth of the land a wrong-built church,
> a domineering, blustering press, a filthy theatre or other house of enter-
> tainment, a hypocrite divine, a publisher of base degree, a mis-managing
> editor, an apish author, a vulgar statue, nor any trickster of any class or
> kind staining the good name of the land. Long live Yankee Doodle, Master
> of Wise Mirth, and First President of Fun![9]

Whether Mr. Yankee Doodle swings his ax at the James K. Polk
administration for its prosecution of the Mexican War or at the
New York City municipal government for its general corruption
and ineptitude, his major concern is always to belabor political
authority when it is unresponsive to the real needs of the people. Thus,
in his "Glorious Triumph of the Ballot-Box," Mathews, the
probable author, reporting on a grand jury investigation which
had discovered that during a recent election convicts had been
transported into New York City in order to cast votes illegally as
citizens, sardonically attacks those politicians who would mute
the legitimate voice of the electorate. He claims he is pleased to
note that the Founding Fathers can rest quietly in their graves, for
their labors in behalf of universal suffrage are more than fulfilled
when even convicts can vote. Indeed, he asserts, we can expect
an even greater justification of our benign and enlightened system
because by next year these convicts may be aldermen and judges
who "may consign other thieves and pick-pockets to the seminary

where they themselves were qualified to discharge their responsible duties." It may happen, too, that the convict population will furnish some of our more practical and enlightened legislators and that the quickest way "to the White House is via Blackwell's Island."[10] Here, attacking the same problem he had depicted in *The Politicians* and *Puffer Hopkins,* Mathews effects a sharper satire by avoiding unwieldy caricature and by resorting to a measured, ironic tone.

Similarly, "The Mayor and the Apple-women," in all likelihood Mathews' work, describes a typical example of the city administration's lack of concern for the welfare of the people: Mayor Brady's decision not to allow people to operate apple stands anymore. This effectually eliminates one of the few opportunities many poor New Yorkers have of scraping together an honest living, but pleases the more respectable, well-off merchants. One of these, a Mr. Jonathan Ledger, writes to *Yankee Doodle* lauding the decree for its "philanthropic" action in removing "a great hindrance to trade." He says, "I have wanted that three feet of the walk for six months every year for my own goods. It would have stood me in good a dollar and three eighths a day which I have lost by being obliged to find storage which would otherwise have stood on the sidewalk as usual." He is pleased that those "Mercenary, monopolizing nuisances, the hucksters," have finally been suppressed.

Juxtaposed against the merchant's letter is one from one of these hucksters, a poor Irishman who, with his wife, has operated a now-forbidden stand. He wonders whether it is "fair play at all fur me an the Ould woman to be turned out o the Sthreet. Shure if the mare turns uz out o the Sthreet, wont the Landlord turn uz into it, its whin the rints is in arrears i Mane."[11] This article is an effective piece of political criticism because it deals directly with the suffering caused the little man by the foolish and often cruel policies of those in government. The satire here is powerful because, like that of "Glorious Triumph of the Ballot Box," it is not based on a method of caricature which unduly distorts reality; instead, it is created by a slight intensification of the folly and injustice of an actual situation. Thus, Mathews' political observations, and, as we shall see, his social commentary, are most successful when he does not stray too far from reality.

V   *Mathews' Political Philosophy*

The fullest summary of Mathews' observations on the American political scene and his most complete statement of the political views based on those observations occur in several articles he wrote for *Arcturus* from 1840 to 1842. In "Political Life," the lead article in the first issue of the magazine (December, 1840), he describes the political system as it ought to be in a nation such as ours; and he juxtaposes against this picture a description of it as it actually is. At its best, our system can attain "a certain naked and Roman simplicity." Thus, "a noble Senator standing on the platform of the nation, in the highest performance of duty, is to us an emblem of whatever is manly and imposing." Similarly, a congress of three hundred deliberating maturely on important questions of polity and national defense is "in such moments of embodied power, the living personation of twenty-six sovereign empires." Mathews declares, "here we breathe the inspiring air of Alps and Allegheny; we are in the high places of the earth."[12]

On the other hand, as Mathews knows, the scene at Congress is usually much less inspiring, and he points out that this is due, in large measure, to a political system which, more often than not, ensures the triumph of mediocrity. For a neophyte politician to advance from a precinct clubhouse to a position of power in Washington, he must avoid independent thought since the party leaders see it as potentially divisive, must practice "a little judicious fawning well-bestowed," and must take zealous part in such activities as carrying a "conspicuous banner in a public procession" or getting up on a stump at election time and shouting "'freedom!' at the top of his lungs" (8–10). Reaching political success through such a process, the American office holder, Mathews believes, has no consciousness of the requirements and duties his position of power entails. He has "no primal sympathy with mankind," no sense of the wants and needs of his constituents. To him, they are mere "painted faces, shadows, automata—anything but men with real problems." This view is directly attributable to the fact that he has been elected through caucuses and committees and has never come into real contact with the voting public.

Moreover, the newly elected congressman has no intellectual capacity nor historical awareness: "With this moral incapacity, exists an intellectual quite as broad and startling. Past ages have not been his study. . . . What knows he of the past? The utmost retrospection of his memory is to the date of some war, some junto or some coalition, which shall serve him as a topic of partisan declamation. Of the present? Not the spirit that moves and animates the masses of mankind, and makes itself visible and audible in amended charters, reclaimed rights, and disfranchized despotisms. No! with him the chronicle of the hour is sufficient for the hour" (15).

The spirit of factionalism, Mathews declares, corrupts our political system, making it rife with demagogues, mediocrities, and thieves. He urges, instead, in "The City Article:—Citizenship," the practice of a citizenship which is too high-minded to lapse into petty squabbles. He speaks of a recent scandal involving misuse of public funds, and he decries the wild charges and countercharges it set off, as each party sought to make political gains out of an unpleasant situation. Mathews sees such a reaction as dangerous, for habitual divisiveness is the sign of an unhealthy community. He believes that Americans should realize that "neither party is to be considered the exclusive friend and champion of truth," for "goodness and right do not inhabit so clearly on this or that side of an accurate straight line, drawn by party wisdom or party honor." Rather, truth is diffused like an atmosphere and pervades all things, all regions, all groups. What is needed, consequently, in American politics, to make it parallel the nature of things is "a qualified and restrained advocacy or opposition."[13]

Mathews does not believe that party divisions should be abolished, but he holds that their excesses should be curbed. One of the most dangerous manifestations of blind adherence to faction is the chicanery practiced by each party at the polling places during an election. Mathews declares that the "Purity of Elections" must be protected: "let the nation speak out: and accursed be he that counterfeits, intercepts, or misinterprets its true, manly tones" (51). To overcome factionalism and its insidious effects, he advocates dedication to country and to principle and awareness of the responsibilities that American citizenship entails. The American citizen is "more sovereign than the highest sovereignty of all old empires; having a mind unawed by past traditions, and cheered to its duty by every hope of the future" (52); as a result, he "should feel called upon to exemplify humanity, and to render to the world the true reading and solution of many vexed problems in government and social life" (52–53). He must realize that he is part of a great tradition of republicans, embracing men like Plato, John Hampden, John Hancock, Franklin, Jefferson, and Washington; and such a tradition cannot be taken lightly or tampered with without terrible effects.

Not only must the native-born American citizen have a sense of the duties he owes his country, but the immigrant to America must not be made a citizen until he has evinced the same kind of awareness. Too often, ignorant newcomers are made citizens through the efforts of political party workers who falsely swear to their character and to their knowledge of the workings of American government in order to make these foreigners easily controlled voters. (Myers says this is one of Tammany's most effective methods of garnering large blocks of the electorate.) Mathews, perhaps inadvertently revealing a dislike and distrust for foreigners, ends this essay by admonishing his readers that they, "the native and natural owners and defenders of the soil, take heed, that by no weak, or idle, or misplaced philanthropy of ours" the national life should be blighted (56).

The consummate display of American factionalism takes place during a presidential election campaign and in "Every Fourth Year" (January, 1841), Mathews satirizes the national follies. He describes the scene as the sanctimoniousness and self-righteousness of the politicians fill the land with cries of outraged decency: "A general uncovering of abuses, corruptions, and enormities of either party takes place, and the whole country is filled with the outcry of exposed culprits, and the odor of governmental gangrenes. The land swarms with declarations and affidavit-makers. The office-holders stand to their arms: and the office-seekers set up an outstanding cry of siege and onslaught."[14]

The presidential campaign has, however, its frightening aspects: the chief one is the rapid formation of hundreds of political clubs, "the ordinary political gatherings and committees cannot satisfy the gregarious propensity. . . . A fraternal, a family feeling springs up among politicians, and they are no longer to be seen singly, but always in troops and herds of hundreds or thousands." Making up these crowds are such clubs as the "Butt-Enders," the "Roarers," and the "Hyaena Club," who "give the world to understand by this designation, that the fury and savageness of their partisanship are by no means to be called into question" (78–79). Such developments as these clubs and mobs are signs of danger in that they are indications of the loss of individuality that results from taking part in the American political process. Instead of thought and reason we find a mob mentality full of potential hate and violence. Furthermore, as Mathews continually reminds us, the whole American way of life is one that was built on individualism; now, ironically, in the name of democracy, that individualism is being lost. Again, to counteract these evils Mathews advocates reason and objectivity on the part of the American citizen. Although such a program may seem to be based on nothing but ineffectual words, Mathews really has little else to appeal to but tradition and common sense; any sort of restrictions on campaigning, other than requesting that the politicians abide by the law, would seem to smack of a totalitarianism alien to everything in which he believes.

One possible means of returning to the common sense that Mathews emphasizes is through a realization on the part of the public and its elected officials that the office of the presidency of the United States "is not, should not be the government of the United States" (81). Mathews sees the public as aggrandizing this office out of all proportion to its lawful powers and as assuming that it has duties which it actually has not: "on this point the public mind has taken a false bias for several years past, and with monomaniac violence to truth, has wrought innumerable evils by neglecting the claims of the other elements of government on their attention" (81). When the public at large neglects local and state government, it is left to be run by the political hacks, who, through patronage and fraud, build up a system of factionalism which, to the detriment of the nation, not only perpetuates itself but proliferates.

Reflecting his animus toward factionalism is Mathews' continued opposition to the idea of using public money to help finance Catholic parochial schools. He believes that, in addition to being unconstitutional, public aid to religious schools works to foment factionalism, for the effect of these schools is to make impressionable young minds see man not in his totality but only in his aspect as the embodiment of some religious creed. Viewing men in such a manner can breed only intolerance and hatred; and, needless to say, it would be abysmally stupid to foster such hatred with public funds. The common schools, on the other hand, free students from religious divisiveness and break down inbred prejudices. These schools are not irreligious, as their Catholic critics claim, for they inculcate children with beliefs in God, conscience, and Savior—and they do it without instilling principles of bigotry. Morover, the common schools inspire the scruples that lead one to speak out "against the oppression of tyrants, the crafts of priests, [and] the violences of wicked men."[15] It seems, though, that through his reference to "the crafts of priests" Mathews reveals something of the Protestant anti-Catholic prejudice which led Catholics to want a flourishing parochial school system. Perhaps Mathews is not so objective here as he would like to think he is.

Factionalism was stilled for a while in 1841, but it took the death of President William Henry Harrison to do it. In "The First Presidential Death" (May, 1841), Mathews praises the orderly process of presidential succession: "this one death, high and lamented as it is, has consummated a great truth, and confirmed our faith in free institutions and free men. A change which elsewhere often wrenches thrones from their foundations has here been wrought with the silence and dignity of a funeral pageant."[16] He hopes it is possible that this reason and order, inspired by tragedy, can persist when the sense of tragedy is gone. The example of the solemn and honorable demeanor shown by governmental officials during this sad time should assure all Americans that their political leaders, what-ever their party, are not "the gross, sinister, and corrupt men they are painted in the harangues of partisan declaimers" (328). There-fore, the public should no longer tolerate such demogoguery; and, if the citizens do not curb it, the parties themselves, seeing the public's response, could curb the political excesses that harm the country by breeding factionalism. A government cannot stand unless it has the respect of its constituents; and, if its officials continue to indulge in mud-slinging, they will lose that respect.

We see, then, that despite his awareness of the shortcomings of the American political system, Mathews does not press for any major overhaul of its mechanics. Rather, he emphasizes inner reform on the part of both politicians and voters, counseling them to act with statesmanlike selflessness and objectivity. Perhaps this seems naïve in the light of our ever renewed awareness of voter apathy and stupidity and of governmental inefficiency and corruption, but we must remember that Mathews was a member of a generation still close to the American Revolution and that his outlook combined nineteenth-century romanticism with eighteenth-century faith in man's rationality to form an almost unshakable optimism, even in the face of ugly facts. We will observe this mentality again when we study Mathews' commentary on social injustice in America.

CHAPTER 7

Mathews as a Social Theorist

I *Literary Nationalist as Social Critic*

MATHEWS' description of the problems on the American scene goes beyond a presentation of the failures of the political system to reveal the injustice which blights the lives of too many of his countrymen who are on the wrong end of the social and economic scale. Endeavoring to ascertain the causes of this social inequity and a means of ending it, Mathews evolves a social philosophy emphasizing self-control, acceptance, and charity. His emphasis on moral rectitude, to the virtual exclusion of legislated reform, may seem unrealistic and, hence, ineffectual; but we must remember that Mathews was a nineteenth-century American democrat; as such, he unhesitatingly placed his faith in the good sense and good will of the individual American citizen. This faith seemed particularly well founded in Mathews' era, for the examples of courage and selflessness in the Revolution and in the War of 1812 were still fresh, and manifestations of diligence and acumen were everywhere evident in the thriving young nation.

His writings which deal with social inequity in America fall, despite some overlapping, into two distinct groups, that of observation and that of theory. In his *Motley Book* sketch, "The Potter's Field," in *The Career of Puffer Hopkins,* in *Moneypenny,* and in several sketches in the magazine of topical commentary, *Yankee Doodle,* Mathews describes the unfair social and economic conditions in which many Americans live; in his *Poems on Man in His Various Aspects Under the American Republic,* and in several essays of social theory in *Arcturus* and *Yankee Doodle,* he evolves the social philosophy which is based, in part, on these observations, as well as on his observations of American manners, customs, and way of life. His last significant statement on social injustice is *Calmstorm, The Reformer,* which presents both his most vivid description of social abuses and his strongest statement of social theory.

II *Pictures of Social Inequity*

As early as his first published works, the sketches incorporated in *The Motley Book,* Mathews evinces an awareness of social inequity. In "Potter's Field," the author, standing amid the graves of the unnamed poor, compares the aura of death in this place with that in the cemeteries of the rich: "here the grim phantom stalks naked; not skulking as in the cemeteries of the rich and prosperous, behind funeral piles, or stealing away from the gaze amid masses of carved marble."[1] He muses that, if summoned from their rest, the inhabitants of the potter's field would form a vast pageant of poverty and suffering.

In his reverie he fancies that these dead wretches do, in fact, arise before him to tell their stories. Implicit in their accounts is a criticism of the wide gap that separates the lives of the rich from those of the poor. A forlorn seamstress laments that she was robbed of her youth and driven to the grave by conditions which permit tailors to "ride in carriages, that poor girls [the seamstresses] might starve." She then hands the author a catalogue of the miserable piece-work wage scale on which she attempted to make a living. He hears, too, the histories of a pauper Negro, some overworked wood sawyers, and many others. Finally, he declares, "a countless throng of faces was before me, men, women, and children—but all of them wearing a certain proof of the deep anguish that cut to the heart and brought them to the grave. Who knew their malady as they pined away day by day . . . ? None! not one!" (18–21).

Mathews' continued concern with social inequity is less successfully manifested in his satirical novel of city life, *The Career of Puffer Hopkins,* in which he provides examples of lives damaged by social injustice. In this work, an attempt to write of New York as Dickens wrote of London, Mathews both satirizes and sentimentalizes the existing conditions to such an extent that they too often lose reference to the world of reality and become a rather ineffectual commentary that is seemingly aimed at moving readers to laughter or tears, rather than at making them aware of social injustice. For example, his satirical portrait of the villainous, miserly landlord, Fyler Close, is too grotesque to be successful social commentary. Drawn as more a ludicrous vampire than a man, Close is too distorted a caricature to be humorous and too much a stock bogeyman to be frightening. We have met no one like him; consequently, he bears no relation to the world we know. Sitting in his home in the bare attic of one of his buildings, munching on dry biscuits and water, the only food he allows himself, and devising plots for milking more money out of his tenants as well as formulating sundry other illicit projects, he moves one to no new social awareness.

The sentimental portrait of a case of social injustice is as poorly done as the satiric. Fob, the tailor who is used by Mathews to evoke as many tears as possible, is simply a catalogue of misfortunes, not a man. Ill and impoverished, pining for his lost love, Fob is confronted by a well-fed rich man who stalks into his room and demands that work be hurried on a suit that he has ordered. Fob, too weak to stand, lies in bed and wearily assents to the man's orders and threats, even though it is apparent that he is being criminally underpaid (95). This sort of vignette, with its almost bathetic caricatures, is not conducive to inspiring readers to reform the social structure which enables injustice to exist. The good poor man and the evil rich man are such stock figures that it takes a fresh treatment of them to hit the audience with any real impact. We do not find that kind of freshness here; instead, we have a formula that is so worn that it has lost any connection with reality and can move only the puerile reader.

Somewhat more compelling are the comments in *Yankee Doodle*, probably by Mathews, on instances of social inequity which belie national ideals. His use of sarcasm as his chief means of attacking injustice and the hypocrisy which often breeds it conveys a sense of sincere indignation which elicits a deeper response from the reader than the heavy-handed caricature and bathos of *Puffer Hopkins*. In "A Scrap of History" he derides society for its sanctimoniousness in punishing culprits whose vices were encouraged by society itself. In this case, "an ignorant negro who had never been taught that he had a soul, killed a man suddenly in a drunken brawl." The black was arrested and held by a jailer who supplements his salary by keeping a rum shop, and he was tried by a judge who gained his seat on the bench by liberally spreading the wealth he had amassed as a successful tavern keeper. The black, of course, was hanged for being drunk; but the ones who had made him so remained unpunished. Mathews ends this short account by remarking sarcastically, "but all this happened on the moon—such frightful mockeries could never have been enacted in a Christian city like ours."[2]

Similarly, the city cares little for another group of the lowly, the mentally ill. In a short item, "Lunatics Taken In Here," Mathews comments on the report issued by the doctor recently appointed to take charge of the city lunatic asylum, where there are nearly four hundred patients. The appalled doctor states that "they sleep two in one bed and on the floor. I have no assistant." Mathews remarks that the Common Council who built this horrifying institution and the grand jury who tolerate it "ought immediately to be placed among its inmates."[3]

The same tone of bitterness and sarcasm is found in the "Live Portrait," drawn presumably by Mathews, of "The Semstress *[sic]*" in which he notes that American society is not functioning as the equitable community that it purports to be. He claims that many rich Americans want to assume a role in this nation similar to that played by titled aristocracy in Europe. Observing the life of the seamstress, he tells the parvenus that their cause goes well, for the "human drudge . . . can work as many hours, subsist on as little, and be as respectful to superiors, in this country as in the Old World."[4] He describes the miserable conditions in which the seamstresses live—telling of their terribly low wages, their long hours, their poor health, their homes in the slums, and the large families they often have to support. It is little wonder, therefore, that they often slip into vice and prostitution. However, this degradation does make for a grafting of the European tradition onto American soil, and Mathews applauds the situation sardonically: "bravo! this is quite down to the lowest European standards, and is indeed encouraging. . . . Patience, Milady Yankee Doodle! If the wretchedness of others can do it, you shall yet be noble" (90). Mathews again considered the problem of the seamstress in his novel *Moneypenny* (1848), in which he pictures her daily life and portrays the brutal employers and the designing lechers who torment her.

III   *Emphasis on Moral Reformation*

Mathews' awareness of social inequity, his sympathy for the poor, and his angry attacks on specific cases of injustice do not, however, lead him to demand a far-reaching reordering of the

American social and political framework. Organized efforts toward the implementation of specific programs of reform he usually scorns as wild, inefficacious schemes to disrupt the very fabric of the American way of life.

In this distrust of plans for pervasive reformation through the reorganization of American society, Mathews joins greater writers of his era such as Hawthorne, Melville, Emerson, and Thoreau. These men also attack social injustice; like Mathews, they offer no carefully contrived scheme for the reordering of society. Indeed, it seems to be typical of American writers of the period to treat social injustice as unsolvable through political or sociological means; instead, they regard it as a manifestation of failings in the human character or in the transcendent forces shaping the world. For example, Hawthorne advocates that man should heed the better promptings of his heart, Melville inveighs against an enigmatic or hostile universe, and Emerson and Thoreau usually prescribe an inner reformation based on self-reliance which they see, actually, as a form of God-reliance that would render any large-scale program of social reform unnecessary and irrelevant. Not possessing the depths of thought and feeling of these men, Mathews simply calls attention to instances of social inequity in the hope that the typical citizen confronted by such instances will endeavor to alleviate the suffering. Mathews, maintaining his faith in the American political and social system, believes, therefore, that the great majority of its shortcomings can be overcome by the good will and by the sense of responsibility inherent in most Americans.

An early statement of Mathews' social philosophy occurs in his essay "The Unrest of the Age" in *Arcturus,* in which he decries the dissatisfaction and the violence that he sees taking an increasingly strong hold over his contemporaries, as evidenced by the ever higher rate of murder and suicide. For some reason, "custom and usage sit hard upon men; and they strive to escape from them by every possible device and self-delusion." Some men find relief in "wild speculation," indulging in "schemes of forming society into parallelograms or rhomboids, and in contriving theories by which man shall get along without any society or organization whatsoever."[5] The restless spirit of the age, as Mathews sees it, either isolates men, making them solitary and discontented, or gathers them into noisy and tumultuous masses who shout for reform and progress and are still utterly discontented. The domestic values are forgotten, as men are found more often at clubs, lectures, or meetings, than at home with wife and family; and, in spite of their fervid attendance at such public gatherings, American men do not find fulfillment.

Mathews sees the prevailing unhappiness as the result of misplaced aims and of a distorted sense of values. The hardships of the age are needlessly manufactured ones, the "bad passions" are idly fomented and encouraged—"we are mad for money, mad for office and empty power." This hunger for money would not be dangerous and spiritually debilitating if we sought it so that we might scatter it among the poor to brighten their lives; for then "the good purpose would sanctify the pursuit." However, these are not the ends for which Americans pursue money; they want only "bond-and-mortgage piled on bond-and-mortgage" (135) and a power which offers little more than the opportunity to add their voices to the loud quarrels of political and religious strife.

Consequently, Mathews regards Americans as a people given to a narrow-minded materialism, pursuing wealth and power which, ultimately, cannot give them the sense of fulfillment they need. More conducive to their spiritual well-being is a life which seeks occasions of enjoyment for the imagination and cultivates the arts and other pursuits in which the imagination is the chief element. Our national troubles and our vague stirrings of disquietude lie, therefore, in the stifling of our imaginations because the human mind cannot be at ease if it is always dealing with facts and the world of business. Instead, the intellect needs something "remote, uncertain, shadowy and boundless," which can act as a "perpetual gratification that cannot be exhausted" (135). He launches into a paean for the great painters and writers who, soothing us when we are disturbed, make our lives worthwhile.

It is devotion to artistic creation and appreciation which can restore us to contentment. Mathews realizes that the arts are not the sole remedy for the evils that beset the nation, but they do absorb faculties and passions which if otherwise directed might create incalculable misery and crime. He concludes by summarizing this major aspect of his social thought: "Of alarmists and preachers of agitation we have sufficient: we need apostles of peace and tranquility. It is necessary that the heart of the age should be soothed and calmed, and its vast activity turned to some better account than place-hunting and money-piling, the uproar of battle, and the mad cries of trade" (137).

Revealing just how strong Mathews' resistance to social change can be is his review of *The Science of Government, Founded on Natural Law,* by Clinton Roosevelt, a work detailing the author's plan for the reformation of society by its division into three segments. These would be a "Creating Order" of production; a "Preserving Order" of law, war, and medicine; and a "Refining Order" of the arts and sciences. Each of these would have its own responsibilities, which would be determined by its own hierarchy of command. Overseeing these three "Orders" would be the "Grand Marshall," a benign leader with, presumably, dictatorial powers. Mathews, who sarcastically styles Roosevelt's book a "new Apocalypse," regards the author as one who, "like all social theorists, stung by the undoubted evils, wrongs and inequalities of society, would fain sweep out of sight whatever it accomplishes of good." He maintains that Roosevelt's theories are misguided because they do not work with the inner man but are attempts to tamper with the mechanism of social order. Mathews believes that all reforms must begin in the mind of man and then make their presence felt in the outer world. To start from the outside and to try to impose morality on man by arbitrary legislative enactments is folly. Moreover, it is a demeaning view of man's nature to suppose that his destiny depends on forms of government or on regulations of fiscal policy. Man's nature rises above such petty concerns; all that he needs is "the hand of generous instruction." Mathews concludes by calling Roosevelt's book "for the most part baleful, volcanic and treacherous."[6]

IV   *The Maintenance of Social Order*

Mathews' distrust of reformers seems to be grounded in his belief that social distinctions are necessary for the maintenance of social order and that any attempt to eradicate such distinctions can only result in chaos and widespread misery. Therefore, any amelioration of conditions of inequity must be carried out within the context of the existing political and economic framework. In a series of four articles, "The Inequalities of Equality," in *Yankee Doodle* in 1846, Mathews, the probable author, echoes Cooper's *The American Democrat* in speaking of the unavoidable social distinctions which exist within the context of political equality guaranteed by traditional American principles.

The first paper on "The Inequalities of Equality" begins with Mathews' criticism of Thomas Jefferson for preaching social freedom. While Jefferson accomplished a great deal in his efforts to bring political justice to his countrymen, as a social theorist "his mistakes [have] led to an infinity of most serious mischief."[7] Jefferson's first great error was in confounding political with social freedom. Political freedom implies political equality which is a good thing; but social freedom does *not,* as Jefferson wrongly believed, imply social equality, which, in fact, can only be effected "by recognizing and setting forth distinctly the different natural character and position of individuals, and thus securing to each one that right of developing and enjoying himself, without which mere political privileges are a curse instead of a blessing." Mathews describes the chaos that would be attendant upon any attempt to enforce social equality:

Force Pat with his hod to dine with the owner of the building where he has his "job," and afterward to entertain the ladies in the drawingroom; draw Mike Walsh [small-time political hoodlum] to the front pew of Trinity . . . take old Invoice, Drawback and Co. every night to the Opera and place them among scented fans and white Thibet cloaks . . . fill a box at Palmo's with Quaker ladies from East Broadway when Blangy dances the Giselle— and you will have a social disorder as unendurable as it would be laughable. (140)

Social freedom, to Mathews, is not social equality but a recognition of individual independence and social inequality. Society's aim ought to be to encourage and promote the growth of interesting and original forms of character, for idiosyncrasies provide life with much of its color and ought not to be regarded with disdain. It is better to have individuality and even eccentricity than ill-advised attempts at bringing everyone to a dead level. The American nation was built on diversity; if one destroys the differences making up the composite American character, much of the vitality of the nation will go with them, and, in their place, banality and disorder will exist.

For a man who claims to admire diversity and individuality and who believes that they should be encouraged, even at the risk of their verging into eccentricity, Mathews reveals himself to be surprisingly intolerant when diversity slightly imperils the framework of order which he envisions American society, at its best, to be. In his second paper on "The Inequalities of Equality," Mathews describes the gaudy scene that Broadway becomes when it is filled with a mass of women strollers in their bright-colored clothes. We might think that he would be pleased by the diversity of the array, but he finds that "this exuberance without taste, this ambition without refinement, is the buffoonery of independence, the poetry of the commonplace, and the very besetting sin of Yankee-doodledom." Dress practiced according to the "immutable laws of symmetry and harmony" is a grand and fine art (156). However, he is appalled at grotesque contrasts of color and style which shock the eye at every turn and which can only be the manifestation of the social disorder and discord, both moral and physical, which are assuming ascendancy over the American scene. Marriages are mismatched, and occupations and positions are in equal confusion; for all the public cares, nobility may be the lackey of ignorance and vulgarity.

Though it would, perhaps, be applicable to nineteenth-century European society with its rigidly defined class distinctions, Mathews' attack on those who do not dress in accordance with "the immutable laws of symmetry and harmony" is out of place in a society in which most people have not been educated in such niceties. Indeed, his condemnation of parvenus and those without money who affect gaudy clothes in an attempt to emulate those of fashion may appear to smack of snobbery; instead, it derives from his desire that social order be maintained. Despite his faith in political equality, Mathews' belief in social inequality is so strong that he apparently finds it necessary as a means of avoiding chaos for this inequality to be manifested by fixed patterns of dress denoting one's social standing.

For all his belief in the inevitability of social inequality, Mathews is a democrat and has faith in the American dream of a fair opportunity for each citizen to advance socially and economically; and he notes in the third chapter of this series that the "lowly of today may to-morrow take rank among the proudest" (178). Anyone in this country, no matter how lowly his origins, has the chance to succeed if he avails himself of it through perseverance and self-improvement. This right, says Mathews, is an inalienable American one, and the only real foundation of distinction is personal merit. Yet, at the same time, his espousal of the American dream is linked, in his final paper, with the reassertion of his emphasis on the necessity of social distinction. Here, Mathews juxtaposes a picture of the audience at the New York Opera House against that of the crowd at a Bowery dance hall. Despite some affectation of European manners and some snobbery, the people at the opera are a group of genteel representatives of the best of American society. There is "more beauty constellated within our little dove-cote of an opera-house than in any theater of Europe," and the assembly is pervaded by a cool, subdued tone and an atmosphere of culture and refinement which "makes itself palpable to the sense." Mathews waxes ecstatic: "there is a feeling of repose, of security from rude and impertinent interruption, a languor of voluptuous enjoyment, very nearly approaching the realization of a pleasant dream." Completing the charm is the relaxed, though brilliant, conversation (186).

Far different, however, is the scene of merriment down at the Bowery where Yankee Doodle claims he is "as great a favorite as uptown at the Opera-House." Despite this claim, Mathews cannot avoid treating the festivities at the dance hall with a tone of condescension, good-humored as it may be, as in his description of the dressing and eating habits of his friend Bill's "g'hal": "Arrayed in a gorgeous yellow shawl, red velvet bonnet trimmed with blue dahlias, and a mazarin silk dress creaking with flounces, [she] sits regaling herself upon an immense piece of cake, an orange, and 'something nice and warm' in a pint tumbler. This slight and graceful repast concluded, Bill introduces his friend Yankee Doodle" (186). Mathews describes her manner of speech, as she says, "in the softest tone at her command, 'glad to see you sir-ee!'" When asked if she has heard of Yankee Doodle, she replies, "Heerd of him! Well, I hain't heerd of any body else!" (186).

The tone in which Mathews delivers his account of the Bowery inhabitants and their entertainment cannot avoid leaving the reader with the impression that the author is patronizing, particularly when the account is delivered in conjunction with Mathews' extremely laudatory description of the people at the opera. This impression is also conveyed when he describes himself leaving the dance hall as "gently quitting this noisy exhibition of some of the more striking inequalities of Equality." It is apparent that Mathews views Bill and Sally as having habits which would make it inadvisable for them to mingle with the opera crowd; for, if there is too much mixing of those with dissimilar backgrounds and modes of behavior, patterns of social order might be upset and all would suffer. Thus, while he advocates equality of opportunity, he tends to believe that it could lead to a chaotic social situation if those who have not taken advantage of their chance for advancement attempt to emulate the way of life of those whose social and economic standing is higher than their own.

V   Poems on Man

Mathews' view of society, with its emphasis on moral reform and the maintenance of order rather than on sweeping programs of social and economic reorganization, leads him, occasionally, into unduly sentimental defenses of existing conditions. This is particularly true of the generally unsuccessful *Poems on Man in His Various Aspects Under the American Republic* (1843) in which the ideas stated in his *Yankee Doodle* essays of 1846 and 1847 can be seen in their early stages of expression. Ostensibly a portrayal of American life in the 1840's, this collection of poems is, in reality, Mathews' overidealized vision of his country; and his view is so far removed from the real America as to reveal nothing about the national scene except Mathews' inability to move from his observations of cases of social injustice to the formulation of a viable plan for their amelioration. In each of the poems, he speaks to a specific segment of society, such as the parents, teachers, or farmers; and he tells that group the responsibilities it must assume to keep America the smoothly functioning social organism it is. Implicit in all the platitudes of which he unburdens himself in each case are the outlines of a philosophy deeply suspicious of social change.

If Mathews apparently would not quite agree with Pope's line, "Whatever is, is right," he would, however, agree with a statement that the social, political, and economic framework within which the conditions of American life exist is right. In other words, poverty, he would grant, is a bad thing, as hunger is a bad thing; but, he would maintain, if they are to be fought it must be within the existing framework. The worst evil that can befall a community is chaos, and the ordered society is built on established rules, customs, and traditions. Therefore, any reform so far-reaching that it would disrupt these guidelines of order is, no matter how worthy the end, potentially more productive of evil than of good.

Ultimately, Mathews' emphasis on the maintenance of order—as in "The Masses," one of the more important expressions of social theory in *Poems on Man*—can lead him to remove, in effect, social progress from the realm of the possible. He counsels the people not to become unduly vehement in protesting what they conceive to be inequities, urging them to "remember Men! on massy strength relying,/There is a heart of right—Not always open to the light,/Secret and still and force-defying./In vast assemblies calm, let order rule."[8] However, he does not advocate inaction in times of acute suppression. When life is rendered painful and meaningless by vicious tyranny, men must arise. It is a time in which there should "be nothing said and all things done," until once more God's rightful sun shall shine.

In this poem, then, Mathews gives us a picture of an ideal world of intelligent, discerning masses—of America as it ought to be. This picture is so unrealistic that to accept it as an achievable goal, or to see it as having any relation to American society, is ultimately to accept unquestioningly the status quo, while, perhaps, indulging in pleasant fancies of how much better everything might one day be. On the other hand, though, it might lead us to assume that such a perfect world will never exist, so why attempt to change things? Our society is not perfect, the reader might think, but no society can be, and ours is good enough in this imperfect world. Consequently, Mathews' vision, if taken seriously, can be dangerous, whether we accept it or see it as impossible; for in either case, the affluent segment of the public which reads poetry will be lulled into inaction. It is pleasant to speak of intelligent mobs who will act only when suppression is intolerable, and then move coolly and effectually. However, such a situation does not exist. The masses are often so downtrodden as to be made stupid and vicious, and to

speak of social change as coming apocalyptically in some righteous
rebellion against monstrous evil is, in American life, to exile it to
the world of fantasy.

In "The Reformer," "The Poor Man," and "The Preacher," we
see aspects of Mathews' social philosophy as it applies to more immediate concerns; and we note his distaste for social change other
than that in his romantic imaginings of the holy war envisioned in
"The Masses." In "The Reformer," Mathews lauds the advocate
of progress, calling him "man of the future," whose "eye beholds
a shore bright as the Heaven itself may be"; but he tempers this
praise by admonishing him to "rush not, therefore, with a brutish
blindness/Against the 'stablished bulwarks of the world" (86). The
reformer's course is that of nature, and his triumph is "assured
like hers, though voiceless and serene." Thus, the reformer must
not be hasty:

> Wake not at midnight and proclaim the day,
> When lightning only flashes over the way:
> Pauses and starts and strivings towards an end,
> Are not a birth, although a god's birth they portend.
> Be patient therefore like the old broad earth
> That bears the guilty up, and through the night
> Conducts them gently to the dawning light—
> Thy silent hours shall have as great a birth!
> (87)

Such a statement, although ostensibly agreeing with reform in
principle, removes it from all sense of urgency and makes the
effort for social change seem somewhat gratuitous, for it asserts
that nature will bring amelioration to pass anyway. Thus, Mathews
advocates little more than acceptance and inaction.

His resistance to change is engendered, in great part, by his lack
of awareness of environmental determinism, as reflected in his
words of advice to "The Poor Man." In this poem Mathews explains away poverty by claiming that it is God's will that some
people are poor and that, contradictorilly, a man is poor because
of his own shortcomings; presumably, then, it is both a blessing
and a just punishment for a man to be poverty stricken. Mathews
offers the poor man some consolation:

> Plant in thy breast a measureless content,
> Thou Poor Man, cramped with want or racked with pain,
> Good Providence, on no harsh purpose bent,

> Has brought thee there to lead thee back again.
> No other bondage is upon thee cast
>   Save that wrought by thine own erring hand;
> By thine own act, alone, thine image placed—
>   Poorest or President, choose thou to stand.
> (92)

In these words, Mathews reveals little understanding of the lives of the poor and deprived. It is comfortable and morally reassuring to attribute the misfortunes of others to their own failings or to a Providence which cannot be gainsaid, but it is also an excuse for inaction. Mathews is adhering to the American pioneer ethic of rugged individualism with its emphasis on each man's making his own way. An admirable philosophy of life, it is not applicable to people who have never had a fair chance to make their own way; and he seems to use it as a justification for ignoring the need for social change. His abhorrence of civic disturbance is manifested when he speaks of the ideal minister in "The Preacher," whom he describes as "Heaven's good workman [who] bind[s] together the house that roofs us on this dear, dear plot of earth" (103). Mathews shows a less than charitable regard, however, for the preacher who stirs up strife:

> Withered be he, the false one of the brood,
>   Who, husbandman of evil, scatters strife:
>   Brambling and harsh, upon the field of life:
> But deeper cursed whose secret hand
> Plucks on to doom the safeguards of the land,
>   Freedom, and civil forms and sacred Rights
>   That conscience owns: he, conscience-stung, who plights
> His voice 'gainst these, should sheerdown fall.
> (102)

Who could such a blackguard be but a reformer whose actions do not fit Mathews' conception of how a reformer ought to act—he is one who, unlike Mathews' idealized version, does not wait for nature to take its inevitable course of social amelioration.

VI   *Reformer as Destroyer*

Mathews' culminating work of social commentary appeared in 1853 in his poetic drama, *Calmstorm, The Reformer: A Dramatic Comment,* in which, despite his bitterest attack on injustice in

American life, he concludes once more—although, apparently, with deeper reservations than previously—that those who would tamper with American society, no matter how noble their aims, are dangers to the nation. While Calmstorm is presented as a tragic figure, admirable in many ways, his unyielding, fanatical zeal makes him both detrimental to the maintenance of social order and too headstrong to effect significant reforms. Calmstorm's moral fervor and courage lead him to failure and early death—ends which are inevitable for him, not because of weakness, however, but because of a plethora of strength and grandeur. Like Othello, Calmstorm's very magnitude leads him to inevitable destruction, but leads him, too, to be invested in an aura of greatness in the midst of disaster.

As the play opens, Calmstorm is presented as a character of unusually large dimensions. He is described by some citizens who await his coming as "a tower where Strength/and Fortitude, and Hope would build their homes." Spying him from a distance, they say, "we look upon a man forth issuing,/As if he bore something of glory from within." His origins are as eagerly discussed and as vague as those of a messiah with supernatural beginnings. One citizen declares: "he lived deep in the west in his youth 'tis said." Another adds: "I've heard, for this I know not of myself,/ From a low, damp and shadowy corner of the city he springs: an obscure haunt."[9] With all these overtones of the coming of some sort of redeemer, however, are hints of the flaw in Calmstorm's character which will lead him to failure. One of the citizens, who recognizes him as one with whom he went to school as a child, remembers that Calmstorm once "fiercely struck the master, charging him/With an untruth in some small word" (5).

The social scene which Calmstorm returns to change is one rife with unfairness, as evidenced by the conversation of a smith, a mason, and a carpenter. The mason says he works ten hours a day with a half hour for meals on a "great darkling pile, with pigeon slips for human habitations." The smith tells how he has just finished working for two nights and a day without rest to meet a sudden order "for chains to bind a rising/In the upriver prison" (6); and the carpenter claims to be "as cheerful as a beggar's hearse" because of the gallows he has just completed for a hanging in the prison yard (7). Furthermore, Mathews provides additional vignettes that show that all is far from well on the American scene. Two beggars describe the wretched hovels in which they live, the rags they wear, and the loved ones who have died for lack of adequate food and shelter. A man, arrested because of the lies of a swindling creditor, is prodded along to jail by a policeman. He protests his innocence and begs the officer to stop manhandling him, but the brute shows no sympathy, stating, "you're in my hands and that proves half the charge" (13).

The manner in which Calmstorm plans to improve social conditions throws him into sharp contrast with his wife, Umena, and his friend, Waning. Calmstorm—brandishing a sword which he claims killed "wasteful" Indians and was "blazed in blood" during the Revolution—swears that he will use it "until the end has come." Waning tells him, "this is a time of peace, and not of war," but Calmstorm answers:

> War! War!—the age of war has just begun!—
> When the rough hands of false and tyrannous men
> May on these guiltless hands be freely laid:
> When so-called popular opinion
> Plays the out-numbering despot with me—
> In passion's name, let passion be the law,
> And set its fiery foot against th' opposer.
> (9)

Waning, the timid, conventional man of the world, responds by advising moderation, saying that "to walk the world in safety takes a prudent foot and a subtle tongue" (11). Umena, however, preaches otherworldliness; and she asks Waning and Calmstorm for their hands so that they can feel a sense of communion with the "Spirit Blest," the "Comforter," that "needs no sword to cleave his peaceful way,/No cunning tongue to be its pleader" (11). Neither Waning nor Calmstorm heeds her words: Waning rushes away, claiming that he must attend to pressing business; and Calmstorm involves himself in the first case of injustice that he spies, that of a beggar who happens by.

The three philosophies expressed in this first scene—those of the ardent reformer, of the conventional man who advocates taking the course of least resistance, and of the religious devotee—are exhibited throughout the remainder of the play, as Mathews depicts them in action, before revealing to his audience which one is best.

It is Calmstorm, however, and his way of facing life which dominate the action of the play, with the views of Waning and Umena being used to provide counterpoint to his own. Calmstorm's desire for a change of apocalyptic proportion and suddenness makes it difficult for him to relate to the actual world. He speaks grandiosely of the coming time when Right crowned in glory shall assume sway over the world, but he is unable to deal effectively with existing conditions. Umena believes that Calmstorm's desire for immediate, overwhelming change is futile, for the evil of the world changes by the workings of "God's light, gentle and slow and single rayed," and "the beauty of this world is bred in single growth" (46).

Her husband's lack of success tends to confirm Umena's view. At a trial in which he undertakes to defend the poor man accused of fraud by his swindling creditor, he effectually antagonizes the already none-too-sympathetic Judge Darkledge by declaiming, in almost Biblical rhetoric, of the evils and hypocrisy of the time and by proclaiming the new world to come when men fit to judge will be on the bench. He calls for God to aid his cause: "break on this court/Thou purer blaze! that judges, soul smit, may fall/Saul-like, in worship" (22). This speech, of course, does little to endear his client to the court. Furthermore, he berates Slinely, the influential newspaper reporter, given to providing slanted accounts favoring the court. Never, though, does Calmstorm address himself directly to the case at hand, which is quickly lost, the poor defendant sentenced to a long jail term. Leaving the court, Waning tells Calmstorm that "you should have bent your knee a little/To the judge, a little would have served you" (23). Thus, Calmstorm has lost a case; and, in doing so, he has made some powerful enemies.

In a similar manner, Calmstorm's ragings and visionings hurt his cause in another action. Hearing accounts of the horrifying conditions under which the inmates at the city insane asylum are kept, he determines to bring them to the attention of the city magistrates, a corrupt group who care little about the welfare of the mentally ill and who see the asylum only as a means of picking up some easy graft money. Although it would be nearly impossible to appeal to the sympathies of such men, still, Mathews implies, they might be spoken to on practical grounds, through the threat of a damaging exposure if the asylum conditions are not improved. Unfortunately, however, Calmstorm does not consider practical methods; instead, he breaks into a magistrates' meeting, waves his sword, calls them dogs, hurls prophecies of damnation at them, and rushes out. The magistrates dismiss him as a madman, and they are not far wrong.

Finally, Calmstorm has made the city powers his implacable enemies, and he seems increasingly dangerous to them because of the mobs he arouses. To stifle him, they start a propaganda campaign, inspired by Slinely, of speeches and newspaper editorials in which Calmstorm is accused of being a murderer, an anarchist, and, perhaps most damaging of all, a man who wants to stop charity. The campaign is successful: the masses turn on Calmstorm and revile him; his friend Waning is frightened and leaves him; and Umena dies. Finally, Calmstorm himself dies of grief, and his cause is crushed. His last words are: "Let the Hope sit by my grave—Umena knows it—alas" (71). It seems that Umena's course, which essentially is acquiescence to the will of God, now appears to him to be the right one. He has taken to heart Umena's final words, reported to him just moments before his own death, "'tis Christ/That heals and saves the world/Calmstorm look up" (65).

In *Calmstorm,* Mathews appears, ultimately, to preach acceptance of existing conditions because, whatever they may be, they are a manifestation of God's will. Calmstorm's compassion is great, and his zeal to reform inequitable situations is admirable; but, since he is too unyielding, his single-minded efforts can only lead to the social chaos that Mathews abhorred. What Mathews leaves us with in this play, with its rather cloying handling of the too readily available message of trust in God, is simply a defense of existing conditions, despite his hatred of their frequent injustice.

VII *Social Views of the American Democrat*

Thus, although Mathews was fully aware that many of his countrymen were victims of injustice and was outspoken enough to comment on this situation, he was unwilling to advocate any far-reaching schemes calculated to create a more equitable society. This unwillingness did not result from selfishness or callousness, but from the very fact that Mathews was an American democrat of the mid-nineteenth century. As such, he had the same faith in his fellows that the eighteenth-century men who founded America had, and he believed in the ability of each individual to better his own lot without the insulting intervention of others. Similarly, he placed his trust in the charity and good sense of the average American, qualities which would lead, eventually, to the amelioration of the more pressing instances of social injustice. Consequently, Mathews viewed those who advocated compulsory reform through legislation as demeaning their compatriots by revealing a lack of faith in them. Like another outspoken democrat of the period, Cooper, Mathews believed that the dignity and honor of the average American might best be protected through the maintenance of a social and political order based on the leadership of the fittest examples of republican virtue. Such an order, he feared, might be upset by reformers whose plans could end in destroying the stability established through common adherence to a set of national customs and traditions and in implanting in its stead rabble-ridden chaos. This situation would create a social condition in which none could be free and in which all would suffer from injustice. Essentially, then, Mathews believed in America, as it had been created by its founders; and he thought that to tamper with its social system would not only damage it but show, at the same time, an insulting lack of faith in one's countrymen and their fathers.

CHAPTER 8

An Assessment

MATHEWS' program was an ambitious one, that of pointing the way toward the development of a distinctly American literature. He tried to accomplish his objective by encouraging others to write of this country, by campaigning for the establishment of conditions in which American writers attempting to create a "home" literature could compete with popular foreign authors, and by producing, in his own right, works which had relevance to the American scene. It is not surprising, given the magnitude of his aims, that his success was only a partial one.

His writings explicitly on behalf of literary nationalism are a body of perceptive observations on the relationship of the writer and his country. Realizing that in a new, democratic society there are few well-established standards of value, Mathews believed it the function of the author to create guidelines enabling his countrymen to ascertain what way of life lends itself most readily to a smoothly functioning social organism and the happiness it entails for all. Similarly, he held that, in order to allow the author to carry out this important role, society must insure him a fair financial return and treat him with a respect commensurate with his important position. Consequently, Mathews' call for a national literature was addressed to two groups: the authors and the rest of the American literary community. First, he urged his fellow writers to deal with native scenes for an American public because only by doing so could they articulate the needs and ideals of their compatriots, while, at the same time, providing them with the inspiration they required. Second, he demanded that an international copyright law be passed, so that our writers would not be forced into unfair competition with cheap reprints of popular foreign books. According to Mathews, the flood of foreign works into this nation stilled genuinely American voices, forced too many of our writers to produce an imitative literature in order to keep alive, and resulted in a taint of dishonesty which disfigured the whole nation. Appealing to the patriotism of his countrymen, he declaimed that

a great nation must have a great literature, and he worked throughout his career to achieve that end.

An American literature did, in fact, develop in the nineteenth
century, but it is problematical as to how much its growth was
prompted by the exhortations of Mathews and by other enthusiastic literary nationalists. Certainly, the great authors of the century
would have written anyway. Indeed, Brown, Irving, Cooper, Poe,
Emerson, and Hawthorne were all writing before the great outcry
of the late 1830's and 1840's. However, Mathews and men like him
did set an atmosphere in which American authors might think
more readily about writing with the distinct purpose of speaking
to their countrymen, an atmosphere which seemed to beg for a
Whitman to sing the American song. Similarly, international copyright was a long time coming, not being enacted until 1891; and, as
noted, a national literature developed without it. Still, the copyright agreement is a necessary protection for writers, and the continued agitation over the years by men like Mathews kept the issue
alive when it was unpopular and doubtless moved the bill closer to
enactment.

Attempting, himself, to carry out the tasks he set for the American
author, Mathews sought in his writings to depict various aspects of
the national experience. A major part of this effort was his attempt
to treat several events of American history in a grand, almost
epic, manner so that it might be impressed upon his countrymen
that they inhabited a land hallowed by heroes and a heroic tradition. Mathews managed, despite some overblown rhetoric in
Behemoth and a fairly cumbersome allegory in *Big Abel and the
Little Manhattan,* to capture the grandeur and romance of America's
history. In *Chanticleer* and *Witchcraft,* he presented with a good
deal of success American heroes of the past as simple family men;
and he thereby emphasized the importance of the homely,
familial virtues, which he believed played an important part in
making America great. Taken as a whole, Mathews' treatment of
American history shows effectively the influence of the past on the
contemporary national scene and imbues the whole American experience with a quality of epic grandeur that he hoped might serve
as a source of inspiration for his readers. Emerson had pointed out
how important it was to the young nation that it develop a literature
of enough energy and breadth to describe adequately its rough-

hewn customs and traditions. Mathews' efforts to aid in the achievement of such a goal antedated those of his greater contemporaries, Melville and Whitman, and show how completely attuned he was to the needs of his time.

In addition to attempting to bring his countrymen to a knowledge of the epic qualities of the American experience, Mathews sought to make them aware of the color and excitement pervading even their everyday lives. By doing so, he hoped to reinforce their consciousness of being Americans who lived in an environment unlike any other in the world and thus to make them a more receptive audience than they had been heretofore for authors dealing with native materials. His sketches of local scenes captured the rhythms of life in New York and its suburbs, and they also conveyed a distinct feeling of life as it was actually lived in that area. Furthermore, in such works as *Big Abel* and *A Pen-and-Ink Panorama,* Mathews, serving as an urban precursor of the local colorists, pictured the interrelationship of the individual and his environment, while characterizing the ways of life peculiar to various segments of New York society. Finally, running through all of Mathews' descriptions of local scenes is a sense of the energy and expansiveness of a young nation moving toward a grand destiny.

Mathews believed that a major part of the American author's responsibility to the growing nation was his role as definer of national values. He had to serve as a cultural spokesman commenting on the mores and ideals of his compatriots and pointing the way, if necessary, toward goals that do honor to the nation and its inhabitants. In carrying out this function, Mathews acted as a conservator of traditional American values and attempted to recall straying contemporaries to the standards of their fathers. Consequently, he satirized parvenus and their imported fopperies; attacked ruthless commercialism, selfishness, and dishonesty; and advocated the simple virtues, moral rectitude, and noble demeanor of America's heroic founders. Thus, even such imperfect works as *Chanticleer, False Pretences,* and *Moneypenny* took on, like Cooper's *Home As Found,* an aura of urgency as they described a society's losing its way and forgetting its better motives.

Similarly, Mathews criticized the political scene in the United States as rife with blind factionalism, demagoguery, and corruption. He juxtaposed this picture of present conditions against that of the early years of the republic when, he believed, politicians were actuated by principles of high-minded statesmanship; and he thus effected a powerful condemnation of contemporary government officials, office seekers, and a too easily swayed general public. Perhaps, in his political satires, Mathews did not sufficiently restrain his whimsy and often created clumsy caricatures; but we must remember that he was responding to the pressing needs of his time and trying to inspire an immediate reaction. In such an effort, gross caricature can often be more effective than restrained wit and careful exposition; but, it seems in this respect that Mathews was catering to mob tastes in much the same manner as that of the demagogic politicians he attacked. More successful, as noted, were such depictions as those in *Yankee Doodle* of the suffering caused real people by the stupidity or dishonesty of those in positions of political power. Thus, Mathews' political writings were not all of the highest quality, but even the unsuccessful were perceptive commentaries on one of the major failures of his time and offered the sound alternative of a return to an effective and honorable system of government.

As a perceptive observer of the national scene, Mathews described numerous cases of social inequity which he regarded as deriving ultimately, like political injustice and folly, from a pervasive decline in adherence to the traditional values of American life. He bitterly excoriated social injustice, calling for a resurgence of charity and selflessness. Still, at the same time, he was unwilling to change the existing political, social, and economic framework. This resistance to change was not the result of timidity or callousness, but was prompted by his faith in the individual American, and in our national institutions and traditions. He believed that, in time, his faith would be vindicated if the existing social order were maintained and if Americans were given a chance to work out their problems within its framework.

Mathews, therefore, was a conservative American democrat who realized full well that the national life had its shortcomings; but, rather than risk overthrowing our principles and way of life through ill-advised reform, he placed his faith in the individual American and believed that the average citizen would work to ameliorate social conditions. This, of course, is the sort of work Mathews performed as a political observer, in that he provided a valuable attack on abuses, while urging that the existing system be maintained, and even strengthened, by a return to earlier standards of virtue.

The America that Mathews showed us was one shifting from a rural to an urban way of life, with all that such a process entailed in changed manners, values, and social organizations. His response to these changes reveals much of the philosophy with which a staunch nineteenth-century American democrat faced the problems of an increasingly complex world. Instead of advocating a different way of viewing oneself and one's relation to the world, as his contemporaries Emerson and Thoreau did, or coming to grips with the hidden evils and ambiguities of the human heart and mind, as did Hawthorne, whose work he admired, or questioning the transcendent powers that may be, as did his friend Melville, Mathews, faced with the same national situation as were these greater men, urged a return to earlier virtues and manners, those of the nation's fathers, whom he saw as living by a code which was truly democratic. His idealization of the American democracy often foreshadowed that of Whitman in general tone, though not, of course, in overall effectiveness. However, Mathews did, finally, carry out a function similar to that of Whitman in describing the past for a new generation in order that there might be established a continuity of national purpose leading to a grand destiny in the years ahead.

Realizing, then, that his America had no well-established social structure and nationally accepted patterns of behavior, Mathews tried to create a framework of order based on the only principles he believed common to all Americans, those he saw in the heroic forebears who had founded the nation—the principles of courage, individualism, and personal integrity. In this way, he sought to fulfill the high obligations a writer has to his homeland.

Notes and References

Chapter One

1. Anon., Obituary of Cornelius Mathews, *New York Dramatic Mirror* (April 6, 1889).

2. Mathews, Letter to George L. Duyckinck, July 16, 1837. Duyckinck Collection, New York Public Library.

3. Mathews, Letter to George L. Duyckinck, November 16, 1839. Duyckinck Collection.

4. Mathews, Letter to George L. Duyckinck, not dated. Duyckinck Collection. Unfortunately, Mathews does not name the museum or churches involved.

5. *Ibid.*

6. Perry Miller, *The Raven and the Whale: The War of Words and Wits in the Era of Poe and Melville* (New York, 1956), p. 80.

7. Mathews, Quoted in Miller's *The Raven and the Whale*, p. 96.

8. James Russell Lowell, *Essays, Poems and Letters*, edited by William Smith Clark II (New York, 1948), p. 201.

9. Mathews, Letter to Evert A. Duyckinck, October 16, 1852. Duyckinck Collection.

10. Mathews also seems to have done some minor work in the New York theater during these latter years. In G. O. Seilhamer's *An Interviewer's Album*, he refers to himself as the author of a comedy, *Broadway and the Bowery* which had a short run in October, 1874. No copy of this play is extant. Further, Mathews' obituary claims that he was the author of a comic opera, *The Great Mogul;* however, the only reference found to a work of this title was in Odell's *Annals of the New York Stage*, which speaks of it as a drama by the French playwright, Audran.

11. Obituary.

12. Anon. (attributed, however, by John Stafford to E. A. Duyckinck), "Nationality in Literature," *United States Magazine and Democratic Review*, XX (March, 1847), 267.

13. William Arthur Jones, "Democracy and Literature," *United States Magazine and Democratic Review*, XIII (September, 1843), 266–79, cited by John Stafford, *The Literary Criticism of Young America* (Berkeley and Los Angeles, 1952), pp. 69–70.

14. John Paul Pritchard, *Literary Wise Men of Gotham* (Baton Rouge, Louisiana, 1963), p. 70.

15. Evert A. Duyckinck, "Cornelius Mathews' Writings," *New York Review*, VII (October, 1840), 430–39, cited by Stafford.

16. Poe called *Arcturus* "decidedly the very best magazine in many respects ever published in the United States." *Complete Works of Edgar Allan Poe* (New York, 1902), XV, p. 59.

Chapter Two

1. Mathews, "The True Aims of Life: An Address Delivered Before the Alumni of the New York University" (Separately published, New York, 1839), p. 9. Hereafter, following the initial footnote for any work, all page references will occur in the text.

2. *The Politicians.* Included in *The Various Writings of Cornelius Mathews* (New York, 1843), p. 119.

3. "What Has Mr. Edwin Forrest Done For The American Drama?" *Prompter*, I (June 1, 1850), 41–47.

4. *The Motley Book: A Series of Tales and Sketches* (New York, 1838), p. 4.

5. "A Speech on International Copyright, Delivered at the Dinner to Charles Dickens, at the City Hotel, New York, February 19, 1842" (Separately published, New York, 1842), p. 12.

6. *Big Abel and the Little Manhattan* (New York, 1845), p. 12.

7. *Moneypenny, or, The Heart of the World. A Romance of the Present Day* (New York, 1849), p. 101.

8. "John Smith, A Convicted Felon, Upon the Copyright," *Arcturus, A Journal of Books and Opinion,* III (April, 1842), 370.

9. *The Career of Puffer Hopkins* (New York, 1842), p. 138.

10. "An Appeal to American Authors and the American Press in Behalf of International Copyright" (Separately published, New York and London, 1842), p. 4.

11. "The Better Interests of the Country in Connexion with International Copyright" (Separately published, New York and London, 1843), p. 6.

12. Mathews' fear of contaminated, anti-American ideas slipping into an America unprotected by copyright seems to have increased with the passage of years. As late as 1883, in an unsigned, rather xenophobic article for the *New York Dramatic Mirror,* entitled "To Deny Copyright Is—Death," he declares of the importation of many foreign books: "the infection of this slush, copiously and constantly operates as a solvent to disintegrate the very framework and fabric of our country itself." The years have done little but make him more vitriolic in his call for international copyright, and he demands that a committee of authors and well-meaning publishers be immediately dispatched to Washington to press

for a law that would stay "the disburdening on our shores of the dazed intellects, the malign and corrupt outpourings and productions" of the lawless, unprincipled, "bohemian word-mongers" of Europe. It seems that Mathews may be overstating his case somewhat here, and showing more frenzy than good sense, but if he is, it is understandable, for forty-five years of relatively fruitless devotion to any cause can make one bitter.

13. "Americanism. An Address Delivered Before the Eucleian Society of the New York University, 30th June, 1845" (Separately published, New York, 1845), p. 17.

14. "An Address to the People of the United States in Behalf of the American Copyright Club" (Separately published, New York, 1843), p. 9.

Chapter Three

1. Although my use of the word "epic" may seem out of place in that it tends to dignify unduly some of Mathews' clumsier, more pretentious efforts, I find it appropriate, nevertheless, because several important characteristics of the epic genre are apparent in them and because an examination of these works in terms of their relationship to the genre establishes a context in which Mathews' aims here can be more readily defined.

In *Behemoth,* and to lesser degrees in *Wakondah* and *Big Abel and the Little Manhattan,* Mathews includes several features we have come to associate with the epic. His heroes are figures of great, or potentially great, stature, endeavoring to carry out heroic deeds on a landscape of tremendous scope. They are representative figures, and, often, the survival of a whole community and its way of life depends on their actions. In *Behemoth,* as in the great epics, divine intervention plays an important role in the outcome of the hero's efforts to save his community. Finally, in all three works Mathews' inflated style is simply an effort to provide the sort of grand language one usually associates with the accounts of the magnificent events treated in epics.

In his use of elements generally found in the epic genre Mathews, obviously, tries to aggrandize the American scene, emphasizing that it, like the European, has its glorious mythology, heroes, and legends. He hoped that an awareness of America as such a place might lead other American writers to deal with native themes.

2. Miller, *The Raven and the Whale,* p. 82.

3. Mathews, Letter to Evert Duyckinck, August 14, 1837. Duyckinck Collection, New York Public Library.

4. *Behemoth; A Legend of the Mound-builders* (New York, 1839), pp. iii–iv.

5. In his notes at the end of *Behemoth* Mathews validates these assertions with quotations from several American archeologists, including

the Reverend Robert G. Wilson, a receiving officer of the American Antiquarian Society; Moses Fisk, author of *Conjectures Respecting the American Inhabitants of North America;* and others. Another who apparently thought the Mound-Builders a flourishing society was William Cullen Bryant, who in "The Prairies," characterized them as "a disciplined and populous race."

6. Miller, *The Raven and the Whale,* pp. 82–83. Curtis Dahl, "Moby Dick's Cousin Behemoth," *American Literature,* XXXI (March, 1959), 21–29.

7. *Wakondah; The Master of Life. A Poem* (New York, 1841), p. 11.

8. Poe, *Complete Works,* XI, 25–38.

9. Miller, *The Raven and the Whale,* p. 141.

10. *Big Abel and the Little Manhattan* (New York, 1845), pp. 1–2.

11. *Chanticleer; A Thanksgiving Story of the Peabody Family* (New York, 1856), p. 4.

12. *Witchcraft: A Tragedy* (New York, 1852), p. 12.

13. Alexis de Tocqueville, *Democracy in America,* edited by Richard D. Heffner (New York, 1956), p. 181.

Chapter Four

1. William Carlos Williams, *Paterson* (New York, 1963), p. 11.

2. "To the Merry Reader." *The Motley Book,* p. 3.

3. "Beelzebub and His Cart," *The Motley Book,* p. 16.

4. "Greasy Peterson," *The Motley Book: A Series of Tales and Sketches of American Life,* 3d ed. rev. (New York, 1840), p. 26. (This edition adds a new tale to the first edition, while eliminating the preface and one tale from the latter.)

5. *Big Abel and the Little Manhattan,* p. 2.

6. *A Pen-and-Ink Panorama of New York City* (New York, 1853), pp. 5–7.

7. James T. Callow, *Kindred Spirits; Knickerbocker Writers and American Artists, 1807–1855* (Chapel Hill, 1967), pp. 149–50.

8. *A Pen-and-Ink Panorama,* p. 11.

Chapter Five

1. "The N. A. Society for Imposture," *The Motley Book,* 3d ed. rev., p. 128.

2. *Moneypenny,* p. 5.

3. *Chanticleer,* p. 25.

4. Miller, *The Raven and the Whale,* p. 277.

5. *False Pretences; or, Both Sides of Good Society* (New York, 1856), pp. 23–24.

Chapter Six

1. Gustavus Myers, *The History of Tammany Hall* (New York, 1917), p. ix.

2. *Various Writings*, p. 120.

3. *The Career of Puffer Hopkins*, p. 10.

4. William Gilmore Simms, "Writings of Cornelius Mathews," *Southern Quarterly Review*, VI (October, 1844), 314–15.

5. *Various Writings*, pp. 111–12.

6. The work of Luther Stearns Mansfield, in "Melville's Comic Articles on Zachary Taylor" *American Literature* IX (January, 1938) 411–18, and Donald Yanella, "Cornelius Mathews: Knickerbocker Satirist" (unpublished doctoral dissertation, Fordham University, 1971) has been instrumental in disspelling the long-held belief (cf. Perry Miller, *The Raven and the Whale* and Frank Luther Mott, *A History of American Magazines*) that Mathews was virtually in control of *Yankee Doodle* through its whole run. Mansfield points out that the original editorial board was made up of George G. Foster, Richard Grant White, and Evert Duyckinck; and Yanella reveals not only that George G. Foster took virtual control of the magazine until Mathews assumed the editorship but that there may have been some stretches in which Mathews contributed little or nothing to *Yankee Doodle*.

Mathews edited a short-lived sequel to *Yankee Doodle*, *The Elephant*, which ran from January 22, 1848, until February 19, 1848. Its title was probably derived from the then current phrase, "to see the elephant"—to see reality, the truth of matters. Like *Yankee Doodle*, *The Elephant* undertook to expose folly and evil through the medium of satire. Frequent targets of *The Elephant* were those which were attacked in *Yankee Doodle*, such as parvenus, corrupt local politicians, and the Polk administration. Also like its predecessor, *The Elephant* used numerous topical cartoons. In addition to these holdovers, however, *The Elephant* had many short, nontopical jokes of the Joe Miller "old chestnut" variety. Too often, the topical satire and ancient quips fell flat; and the magazine failed, both esthetically and financially.

7. Yanella's recent research reveals that there are only three articles that we can definitely attribute to Mathews. They are "Yankee Doodle Comes to Town" (Vol. 1, pp. 3–4), "Mrs. Yankee Doodle at Tammany Hall" (Vol. 1, p. 63) and "General Taylor to Henry Clay" (Vol. II, p. 191).

Among the other contributors to *Yankee Doodle* were Charles Fenno Hoffman, Parke Godwin, Evert Duyckinck, and Mrs. Caroline M. S. Kirkland, all cited in Duyckinck's correspondence, and most notable of all, Herman Melville, whose contributions were discovered by Mansfield.

8. Mathews, "Yankee Doodle Comes to Town," *Yankee Doodle,* I (1846–47), 3.

9. "Yankee Doodle Comes to Town," pp. 3–4.

10. "Glorious Triumph of the Ballot-Box," *Yankee Doodle,* I (1846–47), 107.

11. "The Mayor and the Apple-women," *Yankee Doodle,* II (1847), 83.

12. "Political Life," *Arcturus,* I (December, 1840), 6–7.

13. "The City Article:—Citizenship," *Arcturus,* I (December, 1840), 51.

14. "Every Fourth Year," *Arcturus,* I (January, 1841), 76.

15. "The City Article:—The School Fund," *Arcturus,* I (January, 1841), 119.

16. "The First Presidential Death," *Arcturus,* I (May, 1841), 326.

Chapter Seven

1. "Potter's Field," *The Motley Book,* 3d ed. rev., p. 17.

2. "A Scrap of History," *Yankee Doodle,* I (1846–47), 89.

3. "Lunatics Taken In Here," *Yankee Doodle,* I (1846–47), 163.

4. "Live Portraits. The Semstress," *Yankee Doodle,* I (1846–47), 90.

5. "The Unrest of the Age," *Arcturus,* I (February, 1841), 133.

6. "The Loiterer," *Arcturus,* II (July, 1841), 124–25.

7. "The Inequalities of Equality," *Yankee Doodle,* I (1846–47), 140.

8. *Poems on Man,* p. 82.

9. *Calmstorm, The Reformer. A Dramatic Comment* (New York, 1853), p. 5.

Selected Bibliography

PRIMARY SOURCES

"Our Forefathers: A Series of Poems," *The American Monthly Magazine,
New Series.* I (1836), 453–56, 559–61; II (1836), 233–34.

"Dietetic Charlatanry, or, New Ethics of Eating," *New York Review,* I
(October, 1837), 336–51.

"City Sketches—The Ubiquitous Negro," *Monthly Magazine,* XI (January,
1838), 54–57.

Behemoth; A Legend of the Mound-builders. New York: J. & H. G.
Langley, 1838.

"The True Aims of Life: An Address Delivered Before the Alumni of the
New York University." Separately published. New York: Wiley
& Putnam, 1839.

"Political Life," *Arcturus, A Journal of Books and Opinion,* I (December,
1840), 5–19.

"The City Article—Citizenship," *Arcturus, A Journal of Books and Opinion,* I (December, 1840), 50–56.

Wakondah; The Master of Life. A Poem. New York: George L. Curry &
Co., 1841.

"The City Article—The School Fund," *Arcturus, A Journal of Books
and Opinion,* I (January, 1841), 114–19.

"The Unrest of the Age," *Arcturus, A Journal of Books and Opinion,*
I (February, 1841), 133–37.

"The First Presidential Death," *Arcturus, A Journal of Books and Opinion,* I (May, 1841), 325–30.

"The Loiterer," *Arcturus, A Journal of Books and Opinion,* II (July, 1841),
124–25.

"John Smith, A Convicted Felon, Upon the Copyright," *Arcturus,
A Journal of Books and Opinion,* III (April, 1842), 369–71.

The Career of Puffer Hopkins. New York: D. Appleton and Co., 1842.

"A Speech on International Copyright, Delivered at the Dinner to Charles
Dickens at the City Hotel, New York, February 10, 1842." Separately
published. New York: George L. Curry and Company, 1842.

"An Appeal to American Authors and the American Press, in Behalf of
International Copyright." Separately published. New York and
London: Wiley and Putnam, 1842.

The Politicians. Included in *The Various Writings of Cornelius Mathews.* New York: Harper & Brothers, 1843.

Poems on Man in His Various Aspects Under the American Republic. New York: Wiley and Putnam, 1843.

"An Address to the People of the United States in Behalf of the American Copyright Club." Separately published. New York: American Copyright Club, 1843.

"The Better Interests of the Country in Connexion with International Copyright." Separately published. New York and London: Wiley & Putnam, 1843.

Big Abel and the Little Manhattan. New York: Wiley & Putnam, 1845.

"Americanism. An Address Delivered Before the Eucleian Society of the New York University, 30th June, 1845." Separately published. New York: Paine and Burgess, 1845.

"A Scrap of History," *Yankee Doodle,* I (1846–47), 89.

"Live Portraits. The Semstress," *Yankee Doodle,* I (1846–47), 90.

"Glorious Triumph of the Ballot-Box," *Yankee Doodle,* I (1846–47), 107.

"The Inequalities of Equality," *Yankee Doodle,* I (1846–47), 140, 156, 178, 186.

"Lunatics Taken In Here," *Yankee Doodle,* I (1846–47), 163.

"The Mayor and the Apple-women," *Yankee Doodle,* II (1847), 83.

Moneypenny, or, The Heart of the World. A Romance of the Present Day. New York: Dewitt & Davenport, 1849.

Chanticleer: A Thanksgiving Story of the Peabody Family. New York: Brown, Loomis & Co., 1850.

"Miss Charlotte Cushman's Last Appearance in America," *The Prompter; A Weekly Miscellany, Devoted to Public Amusements,* I (June 15, 1850), 38.

"What Has Mr. Edwin Forrest Done for the American Drama?" *The Prompter; A Weekly Miscellany, Devoted to Public Amusements,* I (June 15, 1850), 41.

"The Theatre in America," *The Prompter; A Weekly Miscellany, Devoted to Public Amusements,* I (June 15, 1850), 65.

"Several Days in Berkshire," *Literary World,* I (August 24, 31, and September 7, 1850), 145, 166, 185–86.

Witchcraft: A Tragedy. New York: S. French, 1852.

A Pen-and-Ink Panorama of New York City. New York: John S. Taylor, 1853.

Calmstorm, The Reformer. A Dramatic Comment. New York: W. H. Tinson, 1853.

False Pretences; or, Both Sides of Good Society. New York: Cornelius Mathews, 1856.

The Indian Fairy Book; from the Original Legends. New York: Leavitt & Allen, 1856.

"To Deny Copyright Is—Death," *New York Dramatic Mirror*, I (June 30, 1883), 6.

"The Late Ben Smith." [Cornelius Mathews.] *The Motley Book: A Series of Tales and Sketches*. New York: J. & H. G. Langley, 1838. *The Motley Book: A Series of Tales and Sketches of American Life*. 3d ed. rev. Boston: George O. Bartlett and New York: Benj. G. Trevett, 1840.

Letters and Fragments. Duyckinck Collection and Stauffer Collection, New York Public Library.

Letters. Houghton Library, Harvard University.

SECONDARY SOURCES

DUYCKINCK, EVERT A. "Cornelius Mathews' Writings," *New York Review*, VII (October, 1840), 430–39. A favorable review of Mathews' early work, given by one of his close friends.

———— and GEORGE L. DUYCKINCK. *Cyclopaedia of American Literature*, 2 vols. New York: Charles Scribner, 1856. Brief biographical sketch of Mathews and short excerpts from several of his works.

MILLER, PERRY. *The Raven and the Whale: The War of Words and Wits in the Era of Poe and Melville*. New York: Harcourt, Brace & World, Inc., 1956. Interesting account of New York literary scene in 1840's and 1850's. Highly unfavorable picture of Mathews as man and author; little scrutiny is actually given to Mathews' work.

PRITCHARD, JOHN PAUL. *Literary Wise Men of Gotham: Criticism in New York 1815–1860*. Baton Rouge: Louisiana State University Press, 1963. Useful aid for putting Mathews' ideas on literary nationalism into the larger critical context of the era.

SIMMS, WILLIAM GILMORE. "Writings of Cornelius Mathews," *Southern Quarterly Review*, VI (October, 1844), 307–42. Uses review of Mathews' work as a vehicle for his theory that American humor does not exist, except for the *Georgia Scenes* of Judge Longstreet.

STAFFORD , JOHN. *The Literary Criticism of Young America*. ("University of California Publications in English Studies," III.) Berkeley and Los Angeles: University of California Press, 1952. Helpful study of the literary movement with which Mathews identified himself. Brief analysis of Mathews' critical views.

YANNELLA, DONALD. "Cornelius Mathews: Knickerbocker Satirist" Unpublished doctoral dissertation, Fordham University, 1971. Excellent study of a major segment of Mathews' career.

Index